T0068222

Labour of Love

A Woman's Journey from Pain to Purpose

AKENNA C. KUBLAL

WESTBOW
PRESS®

A DIVISION OF THOMAS NELSON
& ZONDERVAN

WestBow Press books may be ordered through booksellers or by contacting:

WestBow Press
A Division of Thomas Nelson & Zondervan
1663 Liberty Drive
Bloomington, IN 47403
www.westbowpress.com
844-714-3454

ISBN: 978-1-6642-5144-1 (sc)
ISBN: 978-1-6642-5146-5 (hc)
ISBN: 978-1-6642-5145-8 (e)

Library of Congress Control Number: 2021924017

Print information available on the last page.

WestBow Press rev. date: 03/24/2022

DEDICATION

To my beautifully uniquely made daughters, Dominique & Dejanique. You are my world. May this book inspire you to believe in what I see in you. Thank you for being God's gift to me, through which I was able to see and experience true selflessness, love, friendship, and my ultimate purpose, which is to be your mother.

CONTENTS

AUTHOR'S NOTE

This book is for all women worldwide searching to find their true potential and purpose in life.

When I finally decided to start working on this project, I ultimately began to face even more significant challenges than I thought I had overcome in the past. In those moments, I realized that God didn't only want me to write about something but to walk through it as I wrote. How could I speak to something if I did not go through it? Well, I didn't expect that he would want to have me go through it all. (Man, cries God laughs, it is true it seems ..smile.).

Even though my book will focus on Christian values, as my faith is primarily the benchmark of who I am and all that I do, this book is not targeted only at Christian women. It would be remiss of me to minimize it to Christian women only when I knew nothing about what it meant to be a Christian woman for a considerable part of my life. This book and everything I do will always be for everyone, all backgrounds, ethnicities, and genders. Because the reality is, when I had no one, or when no one knew my name, God loved me and knew me the most, and he held my hand as I went through the ups and downs of life.

As you embark on the following chapters, I will share my

personal journey from childhood, pregnancies, and purpose. I will use the connection of a woman's process from conception to Labour to show you the context of what it means to give birth to your purpose.

Two years ago, God showed me that the term Labour of Love was not just subjected to hand-crafted projects or physical Labour. But it was the very act by which a woman goes through painful situations because as she works hard and pushes through trials for the people she loves, through her Labour, he places the dreams and visions he has set in her heart for her purpose to manifest.

As you flip through the pages of my past, I pray that you use my life as an example of strength, victory, and faith, and most importantly, that you will not only see me in these pages but see yourself, your sisters, your daughters and even more importantly. See Jesus in it all.

Thank you for taking this journey with me. It might be hard to flip through some of it.

But I ask you to open your heart and mind. It was my Labour of Love, my testimony from pain to purpose, just as you shall soon have yours too.

INTRODUCTION

"The very act of giving birth is an example that women are the very producers of purpose through the pain. God uses our bodies to bring forth his purposes on the earth through the men and women we birth. Women are God's vessels that he will use to show the world his Labour of Love."

Akenna Kublal

My personal journey to purpose started at a very young age. Before I even knew what it meant. I always felt different. But I just couldn't put my finger on it. As I grew into adulthood, I realized what I thought would have been a purpose, like a job or a career. It was far from what my true meaning would ever be.

Early into my ministry, I met with a group of ladies I had the privilege of leading in an online women's group. I was sharing with them how I had decided to go ahead with my divorce. And that it had come with much prayer, counsel, and even honestly a little bit of regret that I had allowed it all to get to this place.

After all, I was leading Christian women. I don't want them to think that this should be the modus operandi and that they should run and leave at the first sign of trouble in a marriage. But the truth is, they did not walk that journey with me. No matter what I did, they still won't have a full view of the past 15 plus years of my life. Unless I was to do a PowerPoint presentation for them and give them a play-by-play. Which I was not about to get into.

Very nervously, I revealed to them that I was getting a divorce and that I was the one who had filed for it, fearfully thinking that this would be the end of what was just the start of my ministry. A 'Ministry' I was somewhat thrust into by God, clearly; because I had no clue in my own abilities,as to what I was doing!

After sharing what I had decided to do and hoping that it would not affect how they saw me, I looked at their faces in the tiny squares on the Zoom screen to see how they reacted to me. And instead of what I was expecting. Something shifted.

These women, from all around the globe, some of whom I had never met in person, cried with me, shared their own experiences, and accepted me as someone still worthy of walking along this life journey with them, even though I had chosen this path.

They saw my heart and knew that there must have been reasons, my own, and some not so much my own. That would have brought me to this place.

One particular story I will never forget.

She said, 'Akenna when I joined this group. I was unsure if I could share the parts of me that I did not want to share before coming to this space. But, tonight, after you shared what you did. You set me free.'

Her sweet, honest words remain etched in my heart forever. Whenever I am unsure if I should share my life's story, I remember her words.

As she was guided by my truth, my scars, and my vulnerability that night, So too, do I pray the same for you reading this.

May my pain help you to see your true purpose.

As we move from Labouring to Loving ourselves together.

1

PRECONCEPTION

"Before I formed you in the womb, I knew[a] you, before you were born, I set you apart; I appointed you as a prophet to the nations."

Jeremiah 1:5

The human female is one of the most complex and most robust amongst many species on earth. A woman's ability to act as a birthing machine; for some of us, as a factory! Manufacturing humans, like we really manufacture human beings, how cool?

All the while still managing the day-to-day functions of life, is a testament to a woman's greatness.

Some species don't even make it past birth, like the octopus, that stops eating and wastes away right after laying her eggs, (sorry Sis..)

Thankfully, for the human female species, though we suffer through many plights pre-conception and post-partum, some even before we reach the reproductive stage.

Our menstrual cycle and PMS, hormonal changes and imbalances, and the ever-dreaded menopause make us who we are. These characteristics show the strength of the female human anatomy and how courageous women indeed are emotionally and holistically.

While I am no doctor and hold zero expertise in medicine or the study of the female body, or any medical training besides a CPR and First Aid course, which I have promised myself to renew as soon as I finish writing this book.

It is no secret that regardless of anatomy, gender, sexual orientation, or identification, what we put into our bodies and minds as human beings will significantly impact our health. And well, for the next few chapters, as women, it can directly affect any of our hormonal stages mentioned before and more so if we desire to get pregnant or make a decision to make that step toward having a baby. Or even an unexpected pregnancy can be affected by what we put into our bodies and minds.

What we do, eat, drink, and exercise has a significant effect on us as women in our preconception stage. The right foods, medicines, and hormonal treatments can impact our ability to become pregnant with a baby.

But what about purpose?

What affects our ability to become pregnant with meaning, with destiny, with purpose?

Now I did mention that I am not a doctor, so chances are you knew that we were not going to spend the next few chapters discussing what I knew about having a baby. Which for me would be eating snacks, sleeping, shuffling into jeans that no longer fit, and pain (in that order.)

But I do know a thing or two about giving birth to your purpose, or so I hope, or this would lead to a terrible book review.

But seriously, from my experiences, as painful as they were and some still are, thankfully, these experiences forged through with grit and guidance from the Holy Spirit. Has allowed me to experience life from a different lens and hopefully, I can help you see where God can take you, even though you may not see it right now.

As a young girl growing up in Trinidad, the larger island to the twin-island republic of Trinidad and Tobago.

I had no idea what 'Purpose' Meant. I remember constantly feeling a deep sense of 'un-belongingness.' That would linger with me everywhere I went. I would be the last to get chosen in the schoolyard games. I was not good at any sports, didn't play any instruments, felt like I did not have any talents that were good enough, and lacked the confidence to dream that I could.

My mother and stepfather raised me in a regular-sized, residential concrete flat, government-granted home in Arima. We lived a regular simple life.

My mother took care of the home, and my stepfather worked and provided; and though he was not my biological father, I knew he loved me. And even though he was a great provider, good to my mother, good to me, and later down in life my siblings; I still always felt like something was missing, an emptiness that at the time as a young child I could not understand or explain.

My biological father played a role in my life as best as he

could. He and my mother both separated a few months after I was born.

Their separation came after my youngest (biggest if he stood next to me) brother, whom I adore to this day, was conceived around the same time I was born, just a mere eleven days after my birth.

My mother met my stepfather while pregnant with me when she humorously visited a local police station to inquire about the charges if you were to 'harm someone else.' As she plotted her revenge on my father. I still laugh at this account today, who does that? Well, my mother!

My stepfather, the handsome young constable taking the report and then single father, enquired about her situation and later hired her to be his live-in nanny to care for his young daughter who lived with him.

His daughter's mother had recently migrated to the United States and left her in his care.

Shortly after my biological parents' breakup, my mother and stepfather got together and started their relationship and family. I often jokingly refer to it as a real-life scene of Fran Dresher from the American sitcom 'The Nanny.'

Even though my parents were separated, I remained in close contact with my biological father and would do the whole 'weekends at your father's house' thing that co-parents do.

It wasn't until one day that my mother and step-mother disagreed (to this day, I don't know if anyone knows what it was about, not even them, or they all just kept it a secret from me), and I was prohibited from spending weekends there again.

I was heartbroken, didn't know if it was something I had

done and was just plain confused, as those weekends brought me a sense of joy and completeness that I looked forward to, even though my father was hardly ever there. I enjoyed that time being with my stepmother. Who was far from the stepmother you would read about in the storybooks. In fact, she was the opposite.

My stepmother had no children at the time that I came into her life. It wasn't until I was a little older that she had my brother, who she would tell me, 'come 'hear the baby's heartbeat.' And let me listen to her tummy.

I remember her taking me to the furniture store office where she worked. Busily trotting along with her on the random Saturdays she had to take up a shift or her teaching me how to make macaroni pie with a bit of a hint of ketchup on the top before she put it in the oven for a garnish and that extra taste of sweet and tart that you didn't expect it needed.

I didn't mind that the bathroom or toilet they had was outside, a 'latrine' as the locals called it. Or that the house was wooden, unlike my concrete house back home, all I knew was that when I went back to school Monday, I could brag that I went to my Daddy's house last weekend. As a child, all I dreamt of having was a regular relationship with my daddy, as I saw other kids having with theirs.

The children knew the man coming to all my PTA meetings was not my biological Dad, as he did not look like me (or so my childhood mind and unknown hidden rejection made me believe).

The disparity between living with a good stepfather and a not-so-present biological father affected me more than I knew

Akenna C. Kublal

as a child and into adulthood. The preconceived thoughts and notions I created about myself and my family dynamics pushed me into an abyss of rejection, causing me to feel shy, isolated, and afraid to use my voice.

My mother would recall stories of me being introduced to people. I would answer hurriedly and quietly when asked my name, saying ' Akenna Charlene Samantha Cyrus' as if it was one word. However, they still couldn't hear me because I would often hide behind her legs.

These preconceptions that I felt about who I was or wasn't should have been shut down by positive affirmations from my parents and the adults in my life. However, caught up in their adult situations and possibly never had those things said or instilled in them, and because they came from a generation that maybe, did not even know how to affirm their children.

They did not know or possess the tools at the time to groom me into who I was created to be at that time of my life. Or maybe it was not up to them to even do so.

Instead of feeling secure and loved at a young age, I was left feeling entangled in a web of trying to figure out exactly where I fit in the world and

> Instead of feeling secure and loved at a young age, I was left feeling entangled in a web of trying to figure out exactly where I fit in the world and where I belonged.

where I belonged. And this was all before I even finished primary school.

My step-sister, or eldest sister as I refer to her, was the first best friend I knew.

As an only child raised by a single dad in the 90's, I can only imagine the emptiness, confusion, and rejection she felt.

We both became instant sisters to each other, and with time best friends.

Of course, we would fight like all sisters do and go through insane situations together, like when she took me and walked home from school with a group of boys passing in a big ravine that sometimes flooded with heavy rains, playing hide and seek on our way home. Only to be met by my mother with a belt at the top of the ravine anxiously awaiting us wondering why we did not wait on Dad to come to get us after school as we usually do.

I was only about six at the time, so she took the fall for that incident.

We often recall the incident and laugh at the innocence in our lack of fear for that scenario, and the many adventures we shared as sisters growing up in the Caribbean.

Just as she was about to write her Common Entrance Exam to transition into Secondary School, her mother called to say that she was ready to move to the United States and live with her. At the time, I don't think either my sister or I knew what was happening. All I knew was that she was going on an airplane, and all she knew was that she was going to visit her mother.

Little did I know that my first absolute best friend and a big sister who was supposed to protect me at school was leaving to go to another country and that I would now be an instant only child. In one car ride to the airport and a wave Goodbye, I became the only child in a household that was once filled with running around or sisterly fights to me now having to play school with my assortment of shedding teddy bears from the Chinese toy and variety store.

With my sister leaving and me no longer spending weekends at my biological father's house, my stepfather and I grew closer, and I believe we both filled a void in each other's lives and found solace in what was missing from us both at the time.

I wanted to have a full-time Dad, and he had just given up his only daughter. Yet even though I knew he loved me dearly and I him, and even more so, with the replacement that we placed in each other's lives.

It still never filled the real thing. Especially for me, a young child who had no idea how to process these emotions.

My mother, on the other hand, showed little emotions when it came to things like these.

She said what she had to say to anyone and did what she had to do regardless of who felt anyway about anything.

Growing up in an orphanage from a young age planted seeds of rejection and insecurities in her and unimaginable holes in her personality and life that no relationship seemed to fill, not even ours.

In retrospect, I envision myself living with my mother,

stepfather, and older sister and still trying to fit into my biological dad's life and family unit, thinking that I belonged with my birth dad and confused as to why I couldn't be there.

It was an extremely confusing dynamic and time for a 6, 7, 8-year-old to process. Thankfully looking back now, I know that what they needed to say to me then and themselves was that even though I belonged to both families.

Ideally, the family I belonged to was the family of Jesus Christ.

Our traits, physical and emotional characteristics that we inherit will also be passed on to the children that we bring into the world one day. In the same way, those same characteristics inherently play a significant role in how we will process difficult situations we face and how we work through them to fulfill our purpose one day.

In my mother's case, even though she did not share much about her childhood with us, the stories we heard was that she was given up for adoption because she was not of East Indian race and her mother was afraid that if she took her home, that her legal husband would have known that the child was conceived out of an extramarital relationship.

The other story was that my grandfather raped my grandmother and got her pregnant, so she was not allowed to bring the baby home to her marital home after she was born.

To this day my mother has never truly expressed the truth, maybe she doesn't even know what the truth is, and it still is a sore point in family discussions, as race is often something a lot of Caribbean families find hard to address, in correcting many of the divisiveness that comes in ethnically mixed families.

Before my grandmother passed, I recalled her telling my mother that she 'was sorry', only she knew what that apology was for, and thankfully they were able to share in that healing discourse before she passed, as I knew it meant a lot to my mother, in helping her release some of that past hurt that she had endured and that molded her to be the woman she became.

But even following that, my mother always lacked or withheld the maternal qualities that I envied in the relationships I saw between my friends and their mothers, and the mother-daughter relationships I saw on television sitcoms.

The Mrs. Huxtable types that would lay in their daughters beds, brush their hair and listen to their concerns and reassure them that they were beautiful no matter what issues they faced in an episode.

But as a child, I didn't understand that, that was not real life.

My mother was a great cook, an excellent homemaker, did all the things I believe they taught her in the orphanage to do right, but one thing I don't think they taught her was to have human interactions, especially with those with whom you're supposed to show love to, that is your child.

Now, I know what you're thinking, It would be unfair to her or any human being who is not taught specific qualities to be asked to give it to a person, I mean, if we think about the reproductive experience in a woman, for some women who are unable to get pregnant naturally, they may go to a various specialist to seek treatments or suggestions for how they can get pregnant naturally.

When or if that system or the methods they tried are unsuccessful, if the woman or couple can afford it, they may decide to try either the option of a surrogate or in some cases adoption.

For many of us, when we go through things in our lives or lack a specific ability to do something, God will often use someone or in most cases and more effectively use his Holy Spirit, to act as a surrogate in our lives, to adopt us from our present circumstances to make sure that we get to where he needs us to be.

For me, even though I inherited my mother's looks, and some of her characteristics, as I developed through childhood into my teenage years, God allowed persons to come into my life to act as surrogates to deposit into me in areas where there were deficits, it may have been in the form of a specific teacher who would drop me home after school. Or neighbors who would take you out with them as their child and fill in those gaps that for me was missing in my relationship with my mom.

God will often use surrogates in our lives to make sure that we are not derailed from our future destiny, because of our present lack of what we need then, or our ability to produce something might not be readily available to us in that moment. God knows what we need, and even when we don't have it or have access to it right away, he knows and he sends it in ways he knows is best.

When God is producing something, especially something great, he uses extraordinary ways to bring that forward, despite deficits or rejection, the moments where you paid no attention to what was happening in your life, is when parts of your destiny are being set up and put together like a foundation for where your purpose would be built.

Today my mother and I share a better relationship, and the relationship she shares with my daughters is even better than what we had years ago.

My life and relationship with God have allowed us to start on a new course of healing, and even though it is an ongoing process, what isn't?

I've learned to let go of the idea of perfection and think that I need to meet a certain mold of a mother-daughter relationship with her, to accept that we are mother and daughter. And use our relationship, the good, bad, and the ugly and beautiful parts, to help me become a better mother myself, and to minister to other women and young girls along their life journey's as well.

Now that I too am a mother, and understanding my mother's story has allowed me to view her as a woman of strength. She is a survivor who survived abandonment, failed relationships, rejection and so many other issues in life, but still never gave up on life, and through her not giving up, I was born.

Me, and my other siblings were the purpose through her pains.

2

CONCEPTION

"You never understand life until it grows inside of you."

Sandra Chami Kassis

I didn't come from a 'poor' household, and my parents (all three of them) did a pretty good job at earning and taking care of the bills at their homes. I never really lacked anything that I needed up until a certain age.

As my mother and stepfather started to move closer to getting a divorce. It began to feel uncomfortable for me to go to my stepfather. Our entire relationship started to become strained; as I was constantly reminded that 'that is not your father, go ask your father' by my mother.

Picture me, a teenage girl; already coping with the challenges of 'teen ageism', hormones, finding myself, and now having to muster up the courage to ask my father for necessities.

At the time it felt normal, like ok, I'll just jump in a taxi, head to his stall in the local market, and ask him for my weekly school allowance. Sometimes based on the mood he was in or the sales he acquired; I would get an ok sure. Other times, especially if he was having a bad day (or so it felt to me at the time), he would scold me publicly 'Why did your mother send you up here; I have no money this weekend you know, ask her, ask your stepfather (by name).

On other occasions, if he wasn't there, one of his employees would say to me 'your father is not here you know, and he has (Trini dialect) no money.'

The glaring stares and sympathy for this teenage girl pierced my confidence in a most unimaginable way. I vividly remember one particular vendor often giving me the money that I needed saying 'here when your father comes, I'll ask him back for it.' I am unsure if he ever actually asked him back for it.

Years later when I became a flight attendant, I saw that particular vendor on a flight and was able to offer him an extra seat in first class. I could sense the pride he felt to see me there that day traveling back to Trinidad from Guyana. To know that he once gave a little girl money that she needed to go to school for the week and to travel back home, and now she is here on a flight taking care of him.

I didn't realize then that God had people acting as angels in my life, when other people weren't able to be there for me, in their difficult seasons.

And, in all fairness to my father, he honestly may not have had at times, his struggle with gambling in his earlier years as well as having to take care of another family must have been a true and a very hard burden for him to carry as a man. In the same way my step dad was struggling as a man to take care of his family, as it was crumbling before his eyes.

It was at this time, a seed was planted in my life, (may not have been the best one) but I vowed that I would never have anyone make me feel this way again, or later in life, I would never make my children feel this way either. Whether intentionally or not. That I would go out and get what I needed to get and do whatever I needed to do to never make myself feel rejected for things I needed or wanted again.

At the age of 16, I started working at a local clothing boutique to get cash for transportation for school during the week.

I grew tired of the constant Sunday embarrassment at the market and I knew I could manage working and school. So, I applied on my own and told my mother and she allowed it.

I got the job pretty easily, this particular boutique hired young attractive girls in an attempt to attract customers. I worked on Saturdays, half days on Sundays, and the random public holidays when school was out, or when I would lie and say there was no school so I could work an extra day to make some more cash (lying to go to work, the opposite of adulting...).

Even though it was not in the healthiest environment, my grit for independence and entrepreneurship was birthed there.

Working on the 'drags' of Arima as they called it, the most popular street strip mall in the city at that time. A place where most business owners there were young or middle-aged black men, coming from a life of crime or using their businesses to hide other illegal activities, I learned entrepreneurship (or some might call it hustling) at one of the deepest levels.

It was there I learned how to speak to anyone on the street corner, to one of the city's most famous transgender figures, who would show up regularly there for his alleged sex workers to get their weekly fashions, to soca artistes who would come in before carnival to get an outfit, or to the regular person on the street just looking for an outfit, and me just trying to hustle on the weekend, to make that commission on sales.

I didn't see how God was aligning all of that into my prophetic destiny until later in my life.

You see, we often don't view our 'drags' (or as we call it our pit) experiences as something that can be used in our lives, but whenever I am around people who come from those experiences or may still be there, there is a level of ease I feel communicating with them.

> It was slowly being put in my conception through my own personal struggles and traumas that I had to go through like Joseph in the Bible; both in the pit and in the palace.

I often tell people I can interact with anyone from Presidents to Prostitutes, but that ease did not come overnight. It was slowly being put in my conception through my own personal struggles and traumas that I had to go through like Joseph in the Bible; both in the pit and in the palace.

The owner of the store and his right-hand man were well-known womanizers in the city.

However, the power and money they had at the time erased their actions and it seemed like a normal thing for them to be seen with young girls, using them to glamourize their lifestyle. It was almost praised the way they had young girls parading around as their toys to be seen by all.

There were allegations that he had sex with most of the employees some we personally knew were in relationships with the owner in particular, and we would know this the minute we saw them move up to operating the register.

He was a very authoritative character, commanding respect by the way he walked and interacted with others, but gentle and kind to the customers and female staff, often whispering his sick fetishes in their ears. I recall one particular female with whom he had relations at the time approaching me asking if I would 'join' them sometime. The thing is, they did not know that I was not sexually active. It was assumed that most girls working in that environment would have been, because of the stigma that particular place carried.

In retrospect, I don't even think I was sure what I was being asked at the time, I am not even sure I ever answered.

One Friday evening as we were getting ready to close, his right-hand man who would often throw passes at me, came in to lock up the store. I was in the back-staff area getting my things to leave and he pulled the curtain and walked in behind me. I remember feeling his tall body, his big belly pushed me against the wall and kissed me on the lip.

I was half his size, so all I could see in front of me was a white t-shirt and his gold chain. My eyes were wide open in surprise, hands stiff at my sides not sure what to do. At that moment I remember saying in my mind 'God help me.'

I had never been in any situation like that in my life, I was never told what to do when a grown man kisses you without asking and you're in a room alone.

All I knew was that I felt afraid, and as a child whenever I would feel afraid, I would pray.

I had made up my mind that he would rape me or hit me if I tried to move, no one was there so it would be my word against his, and no one would even care if he did because why was I working there if I didn't expect these things to begin with 'so I thought?

I moved aside and awkwardly chuckled to not seem too 'stiff', still hoping in some way that God would remove me from this situation, as the only way out the store door, was past him; he moved aside and the must-have been almost 40-year-old man said to me the 16-year-old girl Áh like yuh you know!' Again, I awkwardly chuckled, grabbed my things, and bolted through the door.

I couldn't wait to get home. I felt dirty, ashamed, scared and Confused!

That evening I hurried home, showered, didn't eat, and didn't say a word to anyone. I locked that into my past and didn't speak about it until today, as I write this to share with you.

I felt moved to write this encounter, to remind you that even when you may feel locked alone in a room with no key and the enemy standing right in front of you, like me a 16-year-old girl without many words to say, shivering on the inside but trying to put on a strong front, all I could have done at that moment was ask God intimately; in my mind to 'help me'.

And he did.

He moved the enemy, even though he could have taken advantage of me at that moment, because God knows what we can handle.

Even though there are women even some reading this who may have not made it out of situations and may have been raped or molested.

And, Even though sexual penetration did not take place in my situation, it was in fact still abuse.

I blamed myself for allowing myself to end up there, I blamed myself for working in a place like that even though I knew better, and I blamed myself for saying nothing to anyone even when I left the job.

Years later, I still felt some guilt whenever I passed by the location, but the lesson has taught me that even when we do nothing about the dangers facing us in our lives that God will protect us, he is our ever-present help in times of trouble, our shield and buckler as the Bible says.

Even in your life, God can use my scenario as an example, as a moment to be used to immaculately conceive purpose inside of you to help another woman make it through a similar experience or, to teach younger ones how to avoid ending up in those types of situations. In my ministry, and even in my relationships with my daughters and nieces. I can now teach young girls how to be aware of the opportunities they take in search of money.

Or even worse, in search of Love.

The bible holds many fascinating stories of the many travails that women faced. One particularly remarkable story is that of the woman named Tamar, found in Genesis Chapter 38.

Tamar, married to a man named Er, became a widow, and went on to marry his brother, who though after several deceiving attempts to get her pregnant, was also unable to fulfill this desired 'destiny' of her father-in-law.

Tamar would, later on, become one of the women in the lineage of Jesus Christ. Even after being abused, tricked and molested by some of the men she trusted in her life.

Her very pull away from her initial storyline in her life's destiny was what would eventually bring forth her truest destiny.

Which is to be used as a vessel for God's purpose and glory, regardless of the initial situations.

You see, for so many of us, when we begin our life, we think about the path we want to take, as children we are often asked 'what we would like to be when we grow up?' hardly ever thinking that what we want to be, may very well be far away from what God intended for us to be.

While we are thinking of mediocre plans and careers for our lives, God has predestined greatness and purpose attached to our names and bloodlines; if we dare only to perceive and believe it.

At the age of 17, I encountered love, or at least what I thought it was, for the first time.

I was getting ready to finish secondary school, and the charming young man graduated a few years before me.

Very charismatic, he would come into the school regularly, to DJ for several school events.

Being a past student, they would hire him to do school concerts and events and he would hang around as his younger sister was also a senior at the school and my peer.

One day after a school function in the auditorium, he approached me and said 'Say Yes!'

I looked at him lost, thinking he was probably speaking to the wrong person, because I know we never had any other conversations before.

In retrospect, now I often joke that it was a spiritual question I was being asked; and not him the human being, asking me for permission to do what he was going to try to do with me; funny, yes, totally untrue; who knows?

Our relationship started on a very tumultuous start.

Unknowing to me, we started dating while he was in a relationship with a girlfriend of a few years, in a serious relationship at that. When I had never even been in any relationship that lasted more than a few weeks, if you were to count the random two dollar Valentine's day flowers I would receive on Valentine's day at school from 'secret admirers', or in my case an 'admirer' if I was lucky.

My lack of experience and his 'experience with experience' made it a disaster waiting to happen.

Very early in our relationship, he made gestures to have sex with me, and I made it clear that it was something that I was not comfortable with at the time.

I always wanted to wait until after marriage.

After a few weeks of dating, and me saying no, he broke it off with me, and I didn't understand why.

He never gave me any reason or said why he stopped communicating, but I just stopped hearing from him.

I was focused on my exams, so finished up school, and not very long after my mother fell ill and had to have surgery performed.

Somehow, he caught wind of my mother being hospitalized, and we spoke on the phone and he came to visit her.

It wasn't long before our relationship rekindled and soon after I had my senior graduation and he came as my date. The only thing is, he came to the prom with his girlfriend as well.

I know what you're thinking, 'What a mess!'

Well, the High School soap opera only gets better.

Not only did he show up with her, but we both coordinated our outfits, and he came in red to match with me, even though he was there with her. (Hopefully, my daughters read this when they are past that age because I can feel the piercing judgment from them, and you as I type this). ★ Now I did say at the beginning some parts would be uncomfortable to read★.

Our little triangle didn't last very long, she eventually caught onto him and me, and after I had given in and had sex with him the day after my graduation, I was committed to not leave now. I had given up what was the most valuable thing I had at that time. My virginity, thinking it would make him choose me.

No matter the cost, I was not going to be having sex out of marriage, even if the marriage would come in years or never, I was not going to be jumping from guy to guy, I couldn't.. Right?

The thing is, I didn't realize that my mindset had nothing to do with my morals or the fact that I wanted to live this great Christian life.

But subconsciously, I was pushing myself down a slippery slope, to accept what I knew I didn't deserve, because deep down I was afraid that I would mimic what I had seen growing up.

And never wanted to be the woman who moved from man to man seeking fulfillment from them.

I would learn later on in my life, that I did the very same thing, the only difference is I did it with one person, but the damage both to me and others around me would be the same. I tied myself into a lie, based on the expectations that I put on myself to be the 'perfect woman'.

Which for any woman, is simply unattainable .

Let me be clear, I don't think this person was a bad person.

It would be devious of me to slander his reputation without first saying that his actions did not always match the abusive episodes we both played a part of.

It was a sort of Jekyll and Hyde situation. If you know what I mean. However, amid his charisma. He did have a bad temper.

By this time, I was out of school and living the 'adult life'.

He would often take me to events with him that he had to DJ at, and show me off as his pretty trophy wife, and shower me with public affection in front of his friends.

But, behind closed doors; whenever he would become upset or his cheating was uncovered, I would be subject to the hand of his anger.

One year into our relationship, I became pregnant.

Eager to share this news with him and my mother, at the tender age of 18, thinking in my childlike mind that this would make things better for me. I shared the news with him, then my mother.

A few hours later, she told me she was thinking and 'she thinks that I should have an abortion, because she is worried about my future and what is best for me.'

I cried on my way to the doctor.

Three of us in the office, I remember bursting into tears as the needle went into my body with whatever substance they were giving me to start the process.

No one considered asking me about what I wanted at that moment. If I were to be asked, I don't even think I would have known.

I was just a child, looking for love, with a man who was just a boy himself, and here I was, now pregnant with a baby myself. And both the father, and my mother took me to abort the baby.

While pregnant as well with dreams and hopes that my mother was afraid that I wouldn't be able to achieve if I had kept the baby.

What I didn't know then, was that She too, like me, was afraid that I would follow the very same paths that I didn't want to follow, and as unethical and as traumatizing as it would have been. The reality is she was showing me love, in the way she knew how, by taking me to have that abortion, as she did not want me to abort my destiny, whether that may have been to her a career, or tangible life achievements for me.

The paths that would lead me down the road of generational trauma that she had endured because of the bad choices of the women that came before her as well, impacted how she resonated with what I was facing.

But, to protect me from what she thought would hurt me, the protection itself did more damage than the 'danger'. Little did I know, That would not be my last abortion.

Following another one a few years later, I ended up hospitalized due to a bad reaction to my body, which could have resulted in me going into septic shock, if it hadn't been addressed.

I am not talking about this to in any way tell another woman what to do to their body, because like I said at the beginning of this book, my story is for EVERYBODY.

But I will share that the immense grief I felt in years following my abortions, that I had not known was there, is something that I had to work through overcoming, that could have been avoided if I had practiced proper sexual protection methods, and earlier preventative care in my earlier years as a young woman.

The grief, and guilt I felt as a young woman was and still is a real thing for so many women. My advice to anyone reading this, that has dealt with abortion, is to first forgive yourself. God, and your baby has forgiven you. You can set yourself free from the bondage that you, the enemy and your mind has kept you in.

You are free, because God said so.

God sees you; you are still valuable; he has not discarded you. Don't allow any guilt, shame, or anyone's condemnation of you to make you feel or even think that he cannot use you because of that one, two, or five mistakes.

No one is you, therefore no one knows what you faced but you, and God; and his approval and forgiveness is all you truly need to start over again.

Don't allow what you aborted to keep you from becoming pregnant again. And that goes for an actual pregnancy, and also a figurative purposeful one.

A few years later, still back and forth in the toxicity of our relationship, fighting with multiple women; as this person who I shared this relationship with, had affairs with women more than I could count on my hands and feet, with episodes of abuse every time I would try to leave. Even after aborted pregnancies, and me moving in with him. Things still were not getting better.

I had left my parents' home, and moved in with him and his relatives, staying in an apartment downstairs their home, at times having to hide from them, because they too grew tired of our toxic dynamic.

There were times when in my embarrassment for them to see me still being there, even though I knew I was not wanted in the home, I would use the bathroom in a small tub downstairs and discard it later when no one was watching, just so that they would not know I was there.

His childhood may have also played a huge role in what he brought into our lives and mine, and contributed to what I tolerated because I wanted a happy family, and for most times, he was not a bad guy, right? We don't realize how childhood trauma affects the choices and actions we make in our intimate relationships even way into our adult lives.

We were a good-looking couple, and pretty well known in social circles. Not only was I being 'loved' but I also got social status, why would I give this up.

Not to mention that I loved him with every fiber of my being, more than I loved myself, to some extent, more than I loved God....

After years of abuse, and calling friends to help me leave, only to return time after time.

Or running to random male friends to talk to, only to run back to him after a few days, or to go back to my parents, only to run back time after time.

I grew weary, weary with myself and weary with God.

One Saturday night after he had locked me in a room and went out on a date with a woman he was having another relationship with for about 4 years.

I cried until my eyes were swollen. The apartment we lived in had a lock that locked from the outside, so I could not leave.

I went into my purse, looked at the packet of painkillers that I had for my menstrual pain, and chugged over 20 tablets.

I went to sleep, and passed out on Saturday evening, only remembering him waking me up around late Sunday evening.

Still groggy, and completely disoriented, I woke up disappointed that my attempt at this escape did not work.

Blurry vision, I remember seeing ants on the floor, telling him there were ants and him saying to me 'what are you talking about.'

I dozed off again, and woke up Monday morning, still with the after taste of the medicine on my tongue.

In retrospect, I wonder…Why didn't he call the ambulance? Or notify someone else in the home? Why didn't he call one of his relatives, wasn't he afraid I could die? I mean that was my intent for me, yes, But still?…

Years later when we revisited the conversation, he said that he couldn't remember what I was talking about, and he doesn't know why he didn't call the ambulance.

I later learnt that maybe he was in shock, or in some form of guilt or disbelief that I would do that. Maybe he didn't think it was that serious. As many people do when their loved ones have suicidal thoughts, or attempts.

Suicide is something that so many people face, in 2021, even in the church.

The World Health Organization said that out of every 100 deaths, 1 of those deaths are suicide.

Not to mention the many attempts, like mine, that failed.

More than empathy, there is a shame associated with suicide, as if persons who resort to the act are some how weaker than those who don't. Especially in Christian social circles.

I can't tell you the number of times I've heard from people, especially in the church, that suicidal thoughts are an attack from the enemy or some sort of spiritual voodoo that controls a person's mind.

But the truth is, life is hard…. Life knocks you down sometimes so far back that there are moments when you feel like you may not be able to get up again.

There are days and moments when we feel like our circumstances are beyond what we are able to bear or handle.

Unfair things come our way that are difficult to comprehend or explain to the average mind. And there is only so much that the human body, and mind, can endure before it goes into overdrive.

Especially when you feel like you're walking these battles alone. Even though, in truth, we never really are.

I could go off on this whole spiritually righteous, inspirational rant and tell you that suicide is the enemy's mindset.

And yes, don't get me wrong, I am in no agreement whatsoever, with the act of taking your own life, or attempting to do so; but I would be a hypocrite if I did not tell you that I understand that life gets hard! And that no one may understand what you're dealing with sometimes, and there are times, there WILL continue to be times, when you will feel like death may be the only answer.

But, having walked that road myself, and it not working, and seeing what God has done in my life since then; I see value now, in the reason why had it worked, I would have thrown away so much purpose that God had intended for my life.

That the Glory that came after ALL of my trials, did not amount to the pain that I felt during those earlier years of my life.

Because what I didn't see then, was that my suicide attempt, was also an attempt to abort the mission of my purpose.

You see, over time, as life deals up difficult blows; we will feel the urge to abort the mission. Whether it's by suicide, staying in toxic situations, listening to the voices of others more than the voice of God, or just staying stuck. But our Father knows the times and ways to do things in our lives, he does not make mistakes, or allows things to happen haphazardly.

He uses the things that we try to abort in our humanness, even after he has put it in us.

Or, the things and dreams that we try to conceive ourselves.

He uses our failures and disappointments, and our failed conceptions or abortions, even things that we cannot control, our 'spontaneous miscarriages' of life.

To mold us into his perfect seed for HIS conception to begin the process of our journey to move towards our purpose, which is the purpose that he has created us for, not what we see in our natural mind.

Because ideally, what God has for us, is so much bigger than the traditions of what we grew up around, of what we think in our tiny human minds.

His purpose precedes what we think we threw away.

God's purpose cannot be aborted.

What God conceives, our minds, cannot begin to perceive! And there is nothing that we could do in our human attempts to abort it.

3

FIRST TRIMESTER

"As each has received a gift, use it to serve one another, as good stewards of God's varied grace."

1 Peter 4:10

Not very long after my multiple abortions and suicide attempt. I started going back to church with a friend, whose parents had invited me.

It was a breath of fresh air for me and a feeling that I had forgotten that I needed.

Being amongst a community of people who believed in God, and who I didn't have to constantly explain him to, people who were able to see me and speak into my life and see the essence of who I was and where God was calling me to be.

Things were going well, and me and my partner stepped up our committed relationship a notch and he started coming to church with me occasionally. Little did I know that while he was attending services with me, he also started to see someone else, who lived in the same area of the church where I had so comfortably settled in.

So, picture this, me going to this place, for safety, comfort and security from the chaos I was furiously trying to escape, only to have the chaos follow me to where I went for safety.

You see, the enemy literally does not cut us any slack!

If we are honest with ourselves, many times in our lives when we run to places to escape from the things that trouble us, or run to people to get away from the things of the world that cause us trouble.

We sometimes end up in more trouble, even greater at times, than what we were in before.

We should not be running to places, people, leaders, or friends for 'HELP', ultimately, what we need to do is run to God FIRST, and He will direct us to who we need to go to, for that genuine help that we may need. But, the humanness in us, desires connection and fellowship. It is how we were created.

The relationship with the young lady, who also happened to be the person who he was seeing for a few years unknowingly to me. This continued way into my time at that church.. And it became the topic of the youth ministry in the church and literally the scandal of the day in some of our circles.

As a young Christian woman, yearning for help, and thinking I was bringing this man to church to get him 'saved', then having another Christian young lady indulge in this type of 'mess' which is what I call it looking back, tainted my trust from an early age in Christian friendships, especially those with women.

As an 'outsider', I always thought that everyone in church

were 'good people', that somehow, if you knew about Jesus, that you must have been someone I could trust, that you were someone I could pour my deepest secrets out too, and that you were someone I could share my future plans with and you would cover me…I mean, aren't all 'Christians' this way?

Well, boy was I in for a shock! Turns out I was absolutely wrong.

The church has imperfect people too, just like you and me. And I learnt that quite early, in my walk with God.

My partner and I would go to church together, and many times he would slip out and go meet her in the back, or come to church so he could answer an altar call and go stand next to her, while I was sitting in the pews.

The situation grew even more toxic when the young lady would reach out to his family and our close friends to get her side across. Now in her defense, I will say that this man was definitely the problem! Stevie Wonder could see that he was playing the both of us, and because neither of us knew our true worth, we fought against each other ; not even knowing that he also had other women at the side playing us as well.

And at the same time also being physically abusive to us both whenever we would attempt to leave.

Years went by, and the situation continued.

It got even messier when he went off to train to join a military service which required him to be away for a few months.

There would be times when he would be discharged on the weekends, and tell me that he was still in the training camp, but really outside with other women.

My relationship with my parents and other friends and

relatives had become so tainted because I kept going back every time they came to my rescue.

So, I became isolated and spent most of my days locked away in his apartment because he would threaten me that if I went out it would be trouble, and accuse me of being with other men. If I would venture out, I would be greeted with punches to my face, and even choked if I took it upon myself to attempt to leave, or go out with friends.

One day we had an argument and he said to me, to pack my things and leave his place, that he doesn't need anything from me because he had her.

I remember crying, begging him not to leave me, even praying and asking God for him to not leave me.

Because, again, I did not know my worth.

I had no idea that I was being abused, I really believed that If I could just behave myself, if I could just live up to the standard of the type of woman that he was looking for, If I could be everything to this man, maybe he would leave the other women alone and finally just stay with me, maybe he would chose me over all 'the others'.

Being on your own at 19 is not easy.

Yes I could have gone to my parents, with my tail between my legs . But it would have required me to leave the toxic relationship I was in, and the truth is, no one was helping me to do that. And If I was to be honest with myself, I was not serious about getting out either.

When someone is addicted to something, they will do absolutely anything in their power to get it or have access to it.

It's one of the reasons we see the majority of homeless people are current or former drug addicts. They would have thrown away or sold anything they owned or any relationship, just to be able to get the drug they needed for their fix.

And what I didn't realise, and what people in my circle didn't realise, is that I was addicted to an even more toxic substance, more toxic that cocaine, meth, alcohol or any substance, I was addicted to an idea of love, from a man who didn't even love himself, and because I didn't understand how to Love me, and I wasn't ready to accept that Jesus loved me; I convinced myself, that somehow, this was what I needed to feel whole, to feel loved, and to be that, what I didn't have. That my purpose was to fix this man.

I believed the lie that so many women in abusive relationships believe, which is that we can fix the person..which in itself is a prideful stance to take, as only Jesus can fix people. We can only be his aid, but it cannot and should not come at a cost to you.

One day, he needed supplies while he was in training, and I had just landed a job at a local bank. I was proud of myself because I finally had something to do with my time and also in a job that people respected, not to mention it was a huge boost to my confidence.

I was making friends and he was in the base camp so I didn't have to worry about him being physical with me because he was away for some time.

I borrowed money from people to get him things, and I stole from that job, to be able to get him things, and also lived up to a standard that I couldn't have to compete with other women. I needed to live up to this lifestyle that would make him see that I was the better choice.

It was literally one of the lowest parts of my life, where every day felt like 'work', working to win over this person's approval, as the other women he had to choose from, drove cars while I was still taking the bus.

And something that I am still not proud about today. Stole money from a job, so I could be the better choice in his line up.

If I were to be frank, we live in a world where authenticity is traded for filters and pretty lies of the things we did, to make others assume that our integrity is somehow built on the premise of 'this is who I am'.

> It's the same with our relationships with God, we take things to the edge to see how far we can go with sin, before God cuts off.

But, for many of us, like myself, my integrity and who I am now, was birthed from a place of poor choices and not knowing who I am, to seeing where It took me and what I needed to do better if I wanted to improve my life and my character.

It's the same with our relationships with God, we take things to the edge to see how far we can go with sin, before God cuts off.

Some young people might say, "Maybe if I'm not married but I play around a little bit and then don't actually have sex it will be ok, maybe oral won't count as sex?"

But if you play around with fire, the enemy will place you

in hot situations that you will then have to get yourself out of, when God was throwing you life lines all along.

Now, I'm not saying that we won't make mistakes in life, like I have, and I am also not saying that if we make mistakes we get a free pass just to clean them up in the name of transparency.

No, but what I am saying is that sometimes, especially as women, we want things and relationships that are not good for us.

We want what we want, and we are willing to even make a deal with the devil to get that thing.

Think about Ariel in the Little Mermaid, she wanted what she wanted, but it came with a price….. Everything in life, good or bad, comes with a price. And we have to be committed to pay it, whether it's good and we surrender our lives to Jesus, or bad, and we give it over to the enemy, which comes at a price to our soul and our relationship with God as well.

After I stole the money from that job, and resigned, I ended up confessing to what I had done, and eventually paid it back.

I remember when I met with the manager, he asked me, "Why did you steal the money?"

He looked pitifully at me and asked it.. Almost as if he was disappointed in a child, asking " Are you ok, this is not like you.", and he was right.

It wasn't…

When we become obsessed with what WE want, rather than what God has for us, we can end up in a pit of foolish decisions that can lead us to our detriment; oftentimes leading to paths of disappointment, embarrassment and regret.

I was so afraid to be alone… afraid that another person

would end our relationship, or take my place. If I had said ``No, I won't be able to get you those items right now OR I'll use your money to get it," if he had a need.

I was insecure that he would go to her, like he had told me a few weeks before, and she would then take my place, somehow winning me over.

I didn't understand my value, and I was willing to compromise yet again, to be the person this man wanted me to be.

I was competing with the idea that I had to meet all this man's expectations and needs, and if I didn't, another woman would, and he would choose her over me.. Because I was afraid that if he left me, I would just be plain old 'Me;, no one would love me, my family won't take me back.

And the enemy fed off of the lies I had told myself and, like a cancer, played it over and over in my mind, to the point where I would do anything, just for this man not to leave me .

I would make bad financial choices for him, bad sexual choices for him and also; to try to fill some void I seemed to have, that I thought he had to fill. I was placing an expectation on him, to be a fairytale version of the man I wanted in my head, when he had no idea of it.

I didn't realise I was doing the worst thing that any person could possibly do in any relationship.

I was worshipping him.

I had made him a golden calf in my life.. And worshiped him to the point that if he had asked me to give my life for him. I would have.

All because I did not understand the fullness of what Jesus did for me.

And I didn't know that before I tried to Love anybody!
I first had to love myself.

In the year 2008, I received news that I didn't know would have changed my life forever.

It was the beginning of my journey, towards healing.

The beginning towards me realizing that I had a greater purpose on this earth.

I visited my church and told my Pastor that I had found out that I was pregnant and that I wanted to marry the baby's father.

He asked if it was the same young man that visits with me from time to time, and I said yes.

With a snarky look, he looked at me from the top of the rim of his glasses, with his head leaned over to say, "Do not marry that young man, you two are unequally yoked."

I mean, he could have told me something I didn't already know...

I left his office equally puzzled and confused.

Here I was thinking, 'I am pregnant and I want to get married,' emphasis on the 'I', and the man of God is telling me don't do it. The truth can be a tough pill to swallow, especially when you already know that it's exactly what you didn't want to hear, but knew it was the truth.

Eagerly I shared the news with my partner, who was angry that I had gone to the Pastor of the church, in the first place; especially the one where he conducted his Sunday morning love triangle. Not long after this, He told me I needed to stop going to that church because the 'Pastor wanted to get with me'.

My mother, this time around, received the news well.

After I had numerous abortions in under 1 year, and got pregnant again, especially after the hospital scare, we decided I would keep the baby and I moved back in with my mother and step father for a few months so I could have her help.

Pregnancy flew by pretty ordinarily for me, looking back I could barely remember ever being sick, or having any real issues during the actual pregnancy, pertaining to my physical health or body.

But I was still in the middle of a very abusive situation, which did not stop because I was pregnant.

The hitting, punching, kicks in my back, on the floor even while pregnant; continued whenever I would confront him about his relations with other women.

In one incident, I went to a movie with a girlfriend, only to wind up in a vehicular accident at 5 months pregnant, when the emergency systems responded, it happened to be some of his colleagues, one of the women who would later become a mistress in our marriage; they called him and there was no answer.

I was taken to the hospital and by God's grace, even after being pitched meters into a drain at the side of the street, I left the hospital with minor injuries to my leg, but miraculously, the baby was fine.

I had to remain on bed rest for weeks, but it was in that time while my body was healing, it's when my daughter kicked for the first time. She let me know 'Mommy, no worries, I am ok!'

Jeremiah 1:5 tells us, "Before I created you in the womb, I knew you; before you were born, I set you apart; I made you a prophet to the nations." I had no idea that God would send me my own prophet in the form of a baby born out of wedlock, to me, a little 19, by then 20-year-old girl.

I am not labelling my child a prophet, and yes everyone says their children are 'special' or God's gift to them. But I say that she was my prophetic gift from God because, by the very nature of her birth, my life was saved.

She gave me meaning to live again, meaning to get back on the grind as it pertained to my goals, my career, my education and my spiritual life.

I was determined to make her life better than mine ever was.

You may recall me earlier talking about how I pushed myself to never be like what I saw growing up.

Well, this also found its way into my parenting style as well. And also, I was committed to not allowing my daughter to be exposed to the toxic behaviors that I was condoning from her father.

Unfortunately, it took years before I began to see that change, and by the time he had stopped hitting me, she was already too exposed to it, that she was an 11-year-old able to give me advice on what to do, while I was still 'stuck'.

I carried that guilt with me for years, even before we got married and she got to that age. Blaming myself for robbing her of the childhood she deserved, all because I wanted to 'fix this person' and control the narrative of my life.

I would constantly question myself, about ..why I allowed my daughter to grow up in this cycle of toxic behavior?

Time passed, and after she was born, in our usual on and off cycle, I broke up for a week with him. We kept things cordial, and in one instance, where we had a family gathering to attend together, I went with the family as my daughter was a flower girl in the event.

Thinking back, I also think I enjoyed being identified as 'The main girlfriend' even though I knew he had others, and he too enjoyed showing me off and now his daughter as his trophies. But this time I had found out that we were heading back down another long-term affair with someone else, and I was done.

I had moved back into a small room with my mother and siblings, and I was in a much better place emotionally.

I was moving towards true healing from the things that he had put me through for about 6 years, and I had committed that now that I have finally acquired my dream job as a flight attendant, there was nothing that I would allow to come into my life to put me back to that place that I was working so hard to come out of.

I was in the first trimester of my healing journey, and getting to where I wanted to be. I was determined that I was going to move forward with my daughter, with or without him.

Then it happened. At the wedding we attended with his relatives. He proposed.

4

SECOND TRIMESTER

"Can a woman forget her nursing child, fail to pity the child of her womb? Even these may be forgotten, but I won't forget you. Look, on my palms I've inscribed you; your walls are before me continually."

ISAIAH 49:15-16

It's important for us to disciple women about the hard things in life, before we prepare them to be wives.

Submission is great, and a biblical principle to teach. How to keep a home is wonderful, how to get up at 3 am to pray over your home, how to do the Love Dare, or watch the movie Fireproof, and the whole War Room approach is great, solid principles that are proven to work and will bring healing and deliverance to relationships and marriages when applied properly, with the right techniques and support.

But, the things like Emotional abuse, Gaslighting, Physical abuse, Adultery, and the impacts of Trauma on your mind and body, especially in the church and amongst Christian circles, must also be taught. As many couples face these issues with no true outlet for help, outside of seeking psychological therapy. Or, if someone in pastoral support is trained in the areas above to handle or even identify these situations in Christian marriage. A lack of this, often leaves victims feeling isolated and abandoned. And somehow to blame for the reason their situation hasn't changed.

Men too, must also seek to disciple other men, in the ways of how to treat their wives and girlfriends in ways that reflect the heart of Christ as it pertains to men being the head and priest of the homes, as well as honoring their wives as God called them to, as Christ loves the church.

The problem is, we have a lot of people looking forward to a huge dinner party called a 'wedding', and glamorizing the idea of getting married and having a great event, rather than having a healthy marriage that would last and not destroy the both parties and children in the process.

We need to become comfortable in talking about the ugly parts of marriage and relationships, for both parties male and female. And not wait until it's havoc to do damage control, but show young couples and people in general from an early age, that the key to having healthy relationships, must first come from knowing who you are, and having an understanding that

God should guide how you love, and be your moral compass as to how to love, honor and treat your partners.

> If you don't know who you are, you will settle for anything, and you will do anything, to get to keep what it is that you think you're worthy of, even if it's underneath the standard of your true worth.

If you don't know who you are, you will settle for anything, and you will do anything, to get to keep what it is that you think you're worthy of, even if it's underneath the standard of your true worth.

The night of the proposal, I walked out of the ballroom feeling happy that he had finally asked me to marry him, but a part of me knew, the reason I had said yes, was because of the grandiose way in which he did it.

Yes, I was still in love with this man, as toxic as it was, and I was getting everything I wanted, the job I had dreamed of, and he had finally realized my worth, he proposed to me, so he must have!

On our way to the car, I asked him, if he was sure that this is something that he wanted, he said yes... but, I knew that even though it was him proposing to me, and I would be his wife, that the proposal was the only way he knew, he would get me back. There was one Ace left in his deck, and he knew he had to use it.

For generations, there has been an insidious link between religion and abuse of women.

Women in ministry, who serve in the church, who grew up seeing their mothers who were married to the Pastor, and have him come home after Sunday service to abuse mom after dinner.

Only to have the younger women grow up with a tainted view of patriarchy and what submission meant to them as a woman seeing their Christian mother being abused, versus what true doctrinal submission should really mean.

It was easy for me to say yes to his proposal, not because of the audience that was present when he went down on one knee. But, because I believed that it was what I needed to do, to redeem myself from getting pregnant out of wedlock.

And now I could become fully accepted in God's eyes.

Also, to me, it meant that maybe he was finally on the right track, to do right by us, and be the man that I wanted him to be. And, in honesty, the man that I knew he could become, if he truly surrendered to God.

Because like I said earlier, men need other men to disciple them, in the same way women need other women.

Women have book clubs, we have PTA meetings, we have the school bake sales, and all the other types of connect groups where we meet to gather with other women, and allow us to share with one another and help each other grow, vent and even gossip, as 'sinful' as that sounds.

The issue with some patriarchal societal norms, is that men often only gather when they have to do something, or when there is a sports game on etc., so there is hardly ever any real space for community and true vulnerability, with authentic discipleship to take place amongst men, who were not necessarily raised in the church.

Therefore, it results in women having to discipline their boyfriends, fiancés and husbands into who they want them to be. And many times, it comes at a major cost to the woman, because she then ends up having to carry a burden that she was not physically or spiritually designed to carry.

I often wonder about the story in the bible with Abraham and his son Isaac, and what it would have been like, if God had asked the mother to sacrifice him, rather than the father.

Why did God ask the man to do this? And not the woman, his mother. After all, she gave birth to him, Abraham had another son, the test would have been greater had it been the mother.. Maybe?

But, if we look in the bible, especially the old testament, men had the true task, of being the armor bearers in the home, and God led the home as their vantage point to which all decisions were made. The husband being the spiritual guard, or as theologically taught, the 'Priest of the home', would be the one who went before God more than the women did.

In today's society, women are the high priest of the home, because men have fallen at the way side, and allowed the enemy to wreak havoc on families, on their minds, on their views of sex and relationships and also used the word 'submission' to make men feel like its ok to treat their wives, as a door mat, and make women think that they need to keep doing more to achieve the outcome of the husband, or boyfriend they deserve.

Now! This is not in all relationships.

There are alot of men. who are by far, the priests of their home and are walking in steady and solid alignment with the word of God for their families and loving their wives, girlfriends, fiancés etc the right way, the God intended way.

But, in many cases, these men would have either been disciplined by another man whether it be their father, or another mentor.

Or, for some, they may have seen their mother being abused, and made the decision that this is not the life they were going to live.

In most situations, where you see a man exhibiting unhealthy behaviors in relationships and family life, it is because it was what they were taught.

Men need other men to help them understand how to get from pain to purpose, just as women need women to help them do the same.

Because if they don't, they will assume that they can erase the past traumas, issues, and their behaviors, by performing random grand acts to get what they want. Or, by putting the responsibility of 'fixing themselves' on the woman they chose to share life with.

Without true deliverance and surrendering to God and the Holy Spirit, for true authentic transformation in their life. No person, male or female can ever truly be 'fixed'. And as I said earlier in a previous chapter, no person has the power to fix anyone else.

The only way someone can be truly transformed, in any area of their life, is to be renewed in their mind first.

Without proper mind renewal, the change will be temporary,

and carnal, and it will leave room for the enemy to step in, with any little foothold he sees accessible to him.

The painful reality is, we inherit what we see as children. And it can either make us a product of it, or make us not want to be like it, so we revert to other types of Obsessive-Compulsive Behaviors, to not allow this to happen.

And for this relationship, we were those two different parallel subjects, one product of what he grew up in, and the other a product of what she so desperately did not want to be.

After getting married and acquiring our first home, I really started to believe that things were getting better. I was pregnant with baby number two. And I do believe that God was doing a work for us, that allowed us to begin on a path towards healing and changing the course of what we had started out on.

My 'now' husband was still not steady in his walk with the Lord, but I continued to intercede that he would get there. There was no cheating in the relationship for the first time in years.

And we were getting ready to welcome our second child. Also, a baby girl.

Her arrival came unexpectedly. When she arrived, I felt like 'maybe my family is complete' and that, we were going to be the picture-perfect family, And me and my spouse would have this amazing testimony to other couples, and we would bring people to Christ together, about how we overcame so much.

And, we did start doing that. Or at least that's the story I told myself.

Even though he was not in church as much, when we did go to church, his personality would attract everyone in the room, and I would enjoy the attention as well. I would often push him to go to the front and talk to the Pastors, to tell them what he did and who he was, in hopes that they would 'take him in' under their wing, and help him be the man I wanted him to be.

I had this idea in my mind, that I knew I wanted to be someone more than 'this', I knew that God had called me to be something, and it had to be with this man. And if I could only get him to be this version of what I wanted him to be in my head, it would all be wonderful.

I mean we overcame so much, my purpose must be with him. What else would it be?

It's a dangerous thing when we start tying our purpose into people, places and things.

Our purpose should be solely in Christ Jesus, through reliance on the Holy Spirit, and our Heavenly Father who created us.

I can't tell you the number of young women I meet on a daily basis, that I see giving themselves to men who have not yet proven themselves worthy of a commitment to them.

In Trinidad we have a term we say that's, 'Why would someone buy milk, if they could get the cow free?'

And unfortunately, for many women, we give of ourselves

in so many ways, before a man shows us that he is ready to marry us. And, by the time that does come around, whether it's the same man or another, we have already given them so much that there is nothing left to build on.

Except for maybe, Sex.

Sex is something that God created to be between a husband and a wife, a gift of intimacy to be enjoyed between two persons, solely in the context of marriage.

Now, I know the millennials' reading this will try all how to defend the socially acceptable entertaining aspect of sex, and that's ok.

But I can only speak from my experience and the word of God, and let you know that sex outside of a marital relationship, will only be an open door to invite trouble into your life, and creates an appetite for something that you or your partner may not be able to fulfill later down the road, when real life steps in.

The reality is that, a huge percentage of you all reading this book, will already have been sexually active before marriage, and if you fall into that category like me, I want to let you know that it does not make you any less of a candidate to be used by God, or to be able to have a Godly marriage and spouse.

But it will require you to do some soul digging, and go back to your why, as to why you made that decision, and if you feel the urge to, repent before God as I had to do a few years ago, to be able to set myself free from the guilt and shame, I felt from having unhealthy sexual encounters before marriage and outside of a marital relationship.

And in one instance, with someone of the same gender.

Now, I'm not saying that for you to become all judgey on

me, but so that I can let you know that I was a 'sinner, sinner', the reallll kind *laugh*… and that God still… stretched his hand out, rescued me and saved me from the depths of sin and brought me out to be able to use my life, painful experiences and journey through being pregnant with pain and trials at first, to realize that I wasn't just pregnant with pain, but I was pregnant with purpose.

After marriage, our sex life stayed pretty much the same, especially since I thought that we had crossed over into a new life, a new season, unfortunately.

I had forgotten about the verse in Genesis chapter 4 verse 7 that said *'sin crouches at your door; its desire is for you, but you must master it.'*

Less than one year into our marriage, I found out that my husband was cheating on me with a young lady that he had known for about 6 years. It was our first Christmas eve in our new home, and one year anniversary. He had come home from work, fell asleep and she text him, when I opened the text message, they were both arranging the time they would meet in the dorms to have sex before their night shift was over.

I was shattered, here I was, with a baby less than one year old, my eldest daughter who was now starting to get settled from our chaos of prior, in our new home, now married so I can't just walk away. what would everyone think?

I confronted him, and to no surprise, he denied it. And, what did I do next? Well, what any intelligent, growing in the Lord, confident woman should NOT do!

I texted the other woman. Not the best look I can tell you.

In the middle of a woman's pregnancy is the most comfortable she'll ever be as a pregnant woman.

Her second trimester is the place where she becomes settled, comfortable, the baby is developing and she finally settles into the feeling of what it feels like to carry this belly around.

Morning sickness starts to wear off, she stops feeling as tired as she felt in the first trimester, and but more importantly, the baby is now growing at its most rapid stage in the pregnancy journey.

For me, at this stage of my life, just out of a toxic courting experience, and entering into marriage, I began feeling very relaxed in where I was and the relationship.

I also didn't realize that my comfortability did not limit the intensity of the attacks that the enemy had on my destiny.

While I was still comfortable, my purpose and testimony were growing at a very rapid stage in my belly, and the enemy was desperately waiting at the door to enter and rob me of my destiny before I could give birth.

I was changed forever. It was one thing to go through all that I allowed to happen before marriage, but in the marriage, I finally accepted that there was nothing that I could do to change this man, I had lost all respect for him. But, as usual I gave in and still refused to leave.

As women, we get attached to potential a lot.

We enter relationships the same way we shop for groceries to make dinner. We make a list, pick up what we need and use that to prepare the meal that we want, and if we get home and realize we forgot something, we substitute with something else, or simply settle for the meal without it.

The problem is, when we settle in relationships, and accept things during courtship ; then get married, we somehow assume that the person will miraculously change because we said some words in front of the altar.

But true change in anyone, including you and I, can only come through real repentance and authentic deliverance.

Anyone can cry in front of an altar, anyone can jump and dance after being prayed for, but in order to stay safe and in the shadow of God's wings, we need to be dedicated to our process of healing and deliverance, otherwise as I mentioned before, we'll fall back into the traps that the enemy so craftily set up for us. Because he is always waiting at our doorstep for us to leave a door unlocked so he can sneak his way in.

When we become comfortable like a woman in her second trimester, we allow the enemy to sneak up on us, and this, if we aren't careful leaves room for us to fall back into old patterns, let our guards

> When we become comfortable like a woman in her second trimester, we allow the enemy to sneak up on us, and this, if we aren't careful leaves room for us to fall back into old patterns, let our guards down, and put ourselves back into situations that we swore we would never get back in.

down, and put ourselves back into situations that we swore we would never get back in.

Now, don't get me wrong, I am not taking the blame for what my husband did, and I don't think any woman should take the blame for what any one does to her in a relationship.

But the reality is, I knew what I signed up for when I even began the dating journey with this person. What did I expect to happen, in the snap of a finger because we dressed up and had a wedding?

To make matters even worse, after taking him back; two years later. Still married, He cheated again, this time with a former girlfriend.

And, when I tried to leave one weekend, he took a cellphone, threw it at me, and left my ear bleeding. My step father took me to the hospital and then to make a report in the police station.

Only to have to return home the very same night.

The next weekend, while the children were at my mother's.

Some friends invited me out with them, and just like in old fashion, he got aggressive and broke down a door to our home.

Unfortunately, this time was different, I grew tired of fighting this battle alone. Desperation makes you do things you didn't think you would usually do.

I called my Father.

Aggressively, my husband banged at the door in rage, breaking past the latch used to double lock the door, and almost making it inside, all while in the open air, not even considering that neighbors were looking at him.

He was unaware that my father and step father were on their

way. As he entered the door, my father and step father pulled up at the same time.

My father had just lost his wife suddenly to illness. He came out of the car holding a machete or in Trinidad what we call a 'Cutlass', and approached him like a Lion protecting its cub. He shouted 'My wife is already dead. I don't have anything again to live for!'

My step father grabbed the large knife out of his hand.

Then, they both came inside, me hoping we could sit and talk and I would have the chance to explain what was really happening and that they would talk to him.

But instead, he Did what any loving father would do, he intervened, physically.

It was painful to me, to have to see my father get involved in that way, and more so, to see my step father telling me to leave them alone. And if I were to be honest, to see my father put his hands on the man that I loved.

But it also released a burden off of me.

For years I carried the lie in my mind that the enemy told me that I didn't have anyone.

That if I revealed to my relatives and friends what I was going through, and I showed them the truth of what I was facing, they would laugh at me.

My father said something that evening after he dealt him the first punch, that I never forgot... '30 something years my daughter was on this earth, and I never put my hands on her, and now you want to!'

Eventually my step father intervened and it ended. And to

this day, it's still not something I am proud of, or not one of my fondest memories.

But I know, as painful as the memory is, that it was necessary.

I also know that it is what any loving father would do to any man who puts their hands on their daughter's. Saved or not!

It was necessary because it gave my father and step father a chance to be there for me to defend me and say what they needed to say and was holding out on for years, and it gave me the chance to see that I was not alone, and that the enemy had lied to me so much for all these years.

The number one tactic most abusers use to disarm their opponent is isolation.

When they realize you are not alone? It takes away their power.

That time, after the second episode of adultery and violence in the marriage, was the last time I felt alone, or disconnected from either of my fathers. And it was also the last time my husband put his hands on me.

5

GROWTH

"Growth is uncomfortable; you have to embrace the discomfort if you want to expand."

Jonathan Majors

The final trimester or last stages of pregnancy, a woman will continue to experience some of the feelings she had all along in her pregnancy journey. But she would also encounter some new symptoms and changes, as her body expands and prepares herself to be able to carry a larger baby and eventually go through the painful process of childbirth.

For many of you all reading, like myself, would have gone through pregnancies and coming to the end of it, in your final term, it's when you feel your 'heaviest'.

But, apart from the extra weight gain and the growing baby and excitement. It's also when you start to prepare for the welcoming of the baby, and you begin to foresee what life would be like when the baby comes into the family home.

It's an exciting time for the mother as she prepares, but with that excitement she embarks on a journey of learning a new body and ending one season of her life as a single woman, to walk into a new life, of motherhood, carrying inside her a life, a destiny, a living human being, a purpose.

In my years on the job as a flight attendant, I found myself enjoying the most; the time I had to myself.

It wasn't that I didn't love my children, or didn't want to spend time at home. But because of the turmoil that I was experiencing at home, mentally more than anything else, going to work was an escape from the reality of my unhappiness and regret, that here I was, with one cancelled divorce and money down the drain, feeling like God wasn't ready for me to leave yet, not wanting to disappoint my children and not wanting to disappoint our 'circle'.

And ideally, not wanting to live in the assumed shame of being a divorced wife. I stayed and escaped when I could for work.

But in doing so, I missed my kids dearly, so each day, it was a constant pull and tug between me wanting to be at home with my children and involved in their lives full time for that season, but also enjoying my career, and using it as my 'escape' or 'me time' to regroup or at least temporarily retreat from my actual reality.

One Saturday morning, I received a call from the company asking me to pick up a flight that was not on my scheduled roster. It was a Saturday, I could do with the extra money, the girls didn't have school so it wouldn't have affected their schedules and I would be back before Sunday morning. I told them yes, took it up and left like any routine Saturday.

On the way back from the one day trip to the United States, we got into some turbulence and somehow, I managed to lose my balance and hit my knee.

As a mother, and someone who considers themselves slightly clumsy at times, having feel multiple times in public places, even losing a side of my shoe once in true Cinderella fashion at a party. I was used to accidents, hitting myself and falling. This was a simple bruise to my knee, and I went about my business finishing up serving the passengers as we got ready to land.

It was a routine landing, but when I tried to get up from the seat, my knees buckled and I couldn't. I had no history of any previous injuries that I knew of, never had anything done to my knees or legs before, so I knew this was abnormal. The Captain called for a wheelchair for me, and my colleagues escorted me to the transportation to be taken to the hospital.

I remember that night so vividly, as it was such a simple incident, but it was the beginning of a new chapter of my life. I think about the simplicity of it all, and the fact that a small bump on an arm rest, had me taken to the emergency room, which then resulted in me having to do multiple knee surgeries later on within the next Four years. The fact that sometimes God uses the simplest of incidents in our lives, to put us on a trajectory, for a course in life, that we may have never imagined, to this day, still blows my mind. God doesn't always need huge dramatic events to reposition you, sometimes all he does is give you a little 'turbulence' along your path, to bump you into where you need to be.

Following my first surgery, I was told that the tear they thought they saw in my ligaments, was in fact not as bad, and that I had no issues. 'Glory to God'! I thought.... But... it wasn't the case. Later on, after being grounded for some time and being told that I would now have to take a new temporary position in the company, I realized that not only did I still have pain in my knee, but that it was worse than what I had before.

So! The doctors repeated the surgery and the problem was 'fixed', well, fixed to the fact that I ended up with 30 % Permanent Partial Disability to that particular knee, and I was being told that I may never be able to return to flying.

My heart broke, into a million pieces in just a matter of years, the emotional rollercoaster of not only having to have all these procedures done on my knee and leg, compiled with physical therapy, psychological therapy, and having to deal with the issues of life. Not to mention, I was really having to deal with coming to terms that the job I worked hard for, the dream job I had wanted since I was a little girl, was being so easily taken away from me.

And it was beyond my control. And not having control was something I definitely couldn't handle. To make things worse, during the time of having these procedures done, and already being out of work, I started to notice some tiny white dots on my hands, and at the tips of my fingers.

My fingers started to become much lighter than my natural skin complexion, and before I knew it, I was starting to see the same spots, now blotches on my face and arms. Day by day, more appeared and they got lighter and lighter. I ignored it for some time, but eventually I did what every person who had a medical condition that they didn't know about did; Yes, I Googled it!

And to my surprise… It had said, what I thought it would say, Skin Cancer or Vitiligo… (It looked like the latter, but my medical anxiety went with the first). I booked an appointment to see a dermatologist, and she did indeed confirm that it was Vitiligo. A rare skin condition that affects over 2 % of the global population, and that there was no cure. We chatted a bit about my health and medical history, then she recommended that I do some tests to see if I had any underlying Autoimmune issues, as Vitiligo was also considered an AutoImmune disorder. After a few days, the test came back negative, and everything else was ruled out, except one thing. Stress!

The doctor told me that my immune system had been broken down, because of the level of stress that I was under over a period of time, and now, my skin was basically attacking itself and destroying healthy melanin cells, and seeing it as foreign. My husband sat with me in the appointment at the dermatologist office, and silently listened and said nothing.

I left the office, thinking about the years of things I allowed myself to go through, and felt guilty that I had done this to myself. How I allowed my mind and these insane spirals in my life trying to control my destiny, now impact my body… What if it was something else? Cancer? Lupus? Something else that could have affected my health, or my life?

I needed to change things and I needed to start changing them now!

When we hear the term 'growth' we think about moving from one place to a better place, but we often don't think about the 'in between' or the issues that God uses to propel us to that growth.

> When we hear the term 'growth' we think about moving from one place to a better place, but we often don't think about the 'in between' or the issues that God uses to propel us to that growth.

When teenagers or children are growing, we hear doctors talk about 'growing pains', when a woman is growing a baby, she may develop stretch marks, as the skin that once held her body, might need to stretch and expand to be able to carry her and what she carries.

In order for us to get to that place of purpose, we need to understand that purpose does not come without growth.

To be able to carry what we will need to hold at the end, when we get to that place of purpose, our hands need to grow to hold it, our minds need to grow to be able to see it, and our spiritual eyes need to grow to be able to handle it. Without growth, there can be no purpose.

No human being, man nor woman, can access the level of purpose that reaches their full potential without going through a season of growth.

And the truth is, Growth is hard! It sure is...

It would be unfair of me to set you up with promises that each stage of your growth will be leading you up to some grand testimony at the end.

For some people you may face trials that may not get better, that marriage may never reconcile, your cancer may never get better, your child may never come back to life.

But what I do know is that as your mindset changes, and you embrace the fact that your growth is a part of your journey to your purpose, It makes it easier to bear the painful growing pains, and hold onto the anticipation that this is all part of the plan. You begin to see that there is purpose in your present pain, if you hold on to the promises of God and see beyond your present circumstance.

The bible tells us to 'Rejoice!' When Trials come.

Well, I don't know about you, but I can't always find the grit to rejoice when the trials come. But the Holy Spirit does the rejoicing for me.

"In the same way the Spirit [comes to us and] helps us in our weakness. We do not know what prayer to offer or how to offer it as we should, but the Spirit Himself [knows our need and at the right time] intercedes on our behalf with sighs and groanings too deep for words." Romans 8:6 (AMP)

There will be difficult seasons in life, where you might not know what to say, or how to pray about things that concern your heart. But God knows, he sees the growing pains that you're facing. Before you were even born, he knew you would face them, and what they would produce, that's why he oftentimes won't intervene.. But he's there, with you.

Our job is to take those growing pains, and allow them to act as fuel to make the moves we need to make to get to where God is pushing us to be, and to places where we deep down on the inside, feel called to go.

Even if it scares us..

For months, the vitiligo continued to spread, sending me on a downhill slope of depression and even lower self-esteem than what I was battling with before.

As I looked in the mirror every day, the memories of what I once looked like, faded away as the pigment of my skin became lighter and lighter, on my face and the rest of my body.

Still in the middle of a battle with my job and figuring out if I would be able to in fact return to flying or not.

I was approached one day in the office by an employee, and asked how I felt about returning to the air; as there were talks going around that some people may not be sure how passengers would react to my skin.

Standing there Looking at her, my blood ran cold.

I could feel the tears swelling up in my eyes, as I struggled to maintain my composure to answer her confidently, (because by now as my skin progressed, I was determined to not let anyone see me crack under the pressure of what this condition was doing to me, not only on the outside, but also on the inside.)

Not only was I already struggling with being introduced to re-learning what I looked like, and what I could potentially look like if my condition progressed. And here I was also being interrogated about my career choices, to leave the one thing that I called mine, my job as a flight attendant, not because of my knee injury, or because of any other legitimate reason, but because of my skin.

I puffed up my chest, and told her 'No, I'll be fine!'

She recommended that I see a dermatologist, then went on to give suggestions on how I could conceal my vitiligo if I was allowed to return to work. I don't remember a more embarrassing moment in my Vitiligo journey, it was new, something I wasn't prepared for. And I had to accept that this would be something I may have to deal with for the rest of my life. Questions and suggestions like this.

Throughout my Vitiligo journey, I have heard some of the weirdest suggestions and comments, I've been told It looks like burns, that it looks like a galaxy, that it looks like a cow.

I've been told all of what I could drink, all the herbal remedies 'which I think I've tried'.

All the creams I should try, that I should travel to Cuba and these other countries for treatment.

How my diet should change and all that I should 'do' to get rid of my vitiligo. I've been told to anoint my hands each day and pray, because the skin condition was not from God.

And, who am I to say, that these suggestions did not come from a place of love and true discernment. I can't..

But what I can say is that my journey with Vitiligo is something that God used in my life, to give me the boost I needed to grow in my faith and to understand his heart, and the love he has for us as his children. For That he loved me, enough to give his son for me in spite of all that I had done.. The times I ignored his voice, that even through it all he saw 'Me!'

Having to wake up every morning and look in the mirror each day, seeing my skin slowly fading away, having my youngest daughter ask me to not pick her up from school, because she did not want the kids to ask her about her 'Mummy's skin' anymore; shattered me to pieces many times.

But recognising that people really did not understand much about the condition as I did, provided an opportunity for me to not only educate my children on what was happening to my body, but also a unique opportunity to teach them about true self love.

We live in a time where so many things are filtered to make us see perfection, Especially image.

Picture me, already insecure at the brim of all the adultery, comparing myself to each woman that I thought in my mind had something better than me, something prettier than I had, why he chose to go each time, and now I have something that makes me 'ugly' or strange looking.

I expected my confidence to hit a downward slope. It may very well be that my skin condition came from the enemy, I can't say.

Just like I can't say why someone who has cancer won't get healing each and every time.

But what I do know, what I've seen in my own life… is that what the enemy meant for evil, God WILL turn around for YOUR good!

And his Glory!! And he has been using my vitiligo story to inspire many around the world.

Not only is growth painful and uncomfortable. But it also comes with no warning to the candidate or the shoot being cultivated.

In the case of a woman. Pregnant with purpose, her growth happens over the course of her life, from the sensitive moments in her childhood, to the adolescent trials she will face during puberty and the relational lessons she will learn as she enters adulthood.

For me, most of the growth in my life came not by fertilizing, but the shedding of the old me, the person I thought I needed to be, to fit into certain circles. To meet the expectations of what a perfect wife and mother was, and to be accepted by God.

It wasn't until I relearned what it meant to truly accept myself. Just as I was, imperfections and all, through my journey with Vitiligo and losing the career that I thought defined me.

Was when I realized that God is not concerned with the things that concern us in order for him to place purpose on the inside of us.

God places our purpose inside us, even before we were born. He does not need our approval, or our consent to put it on the inside of us.

What he does need is our response. Our response to say yes to the calling on our lives to open our hands and be ready to receive what he would place in it, if we would only be ready to accept.

Realizing that growth is not there to harm us, or intentionally bring pain into our lives, but it happens to teach us how to be faithful in pain.

I know that sounds a bit cynical to some of you all. But, think about what women are taught when doing birth training weeks or months even before actually going into Labour.

A Birth Coach or a Doula would help them learn the tools

and techniques of how-to breathe during labour, how to respond when the baby is coming out etc. And this happens way before there are any signs of physical labour. This is because we never know when the baby will come.

In our purpose journey, God will not give us a deadline or a specific time when he will reveal our true purpose to us. But our job is to remain faithfully committed to where we are at doing the painful moments, and to keep seeking him even when we don't feel like he may be even there. Because he is.

> In our purpose journey, God will not give us a deadline or a specific time when he will reveal our true purpose to us. But our job is to remain faithfully committed to where we are at doing the painful moments, and to keep seeking him even when we don't feel like he may be even there. Because he is.

Understanding that even when we have painful seasons in our life, times when we feel like no one gets it or no one understands, is when God is there the most with us.

Just as a baby feels safe in a mother's womb, without even seeing what that mother looks like. So too, can you feel safe in your Father's arms, knowing that he is with you during these 'growth moments'. And throughout life, as seasons change, so too will the growing pains change, and look different. But what remains constant is God's presence and his hand upon your life, and his Faithfulness to see you through.

6

PREPARATION

"You prepare a table before me in the presence of my enemies. You anoint my head with oil; my cup overflows."

Psalm 23:5 NIV

Before I even knew it, five years had passed, and I was yet to return to flying. Thousands of dollars spent on legal fees in hopes that I would find some sort of recourse, and that I could get them to 'pay' for what they had done to me. Countless Medical bills and treatments, and by now my Vitiligo was covering about 75 % of my body, in different blotches all over my body.

Surely, my life won't get any worse than this. But, in the blink of an eye. It did.

My husband had now started working in a new division of his job, and they were having their first Christmas Dinner Party. As usual, he was the go-to person for DJing, so we packed up early, got my sister to come over and babysit, but something felt off. I noticed that even though I was making plans to go, and put things in place to be there, that he never really invited me with him that weekend.

He had mentioned it, casually in conversation, but never officially said 'I want you to come with me?'

'Girl, Don't overthink it'! I told myself. But in true form and fashion, I over-thought it!

Before we left, I asked him, 'How come you never really asked me to come with you, do you want me to come?' he asked nonchalantly. 'It's up to you!'. Ooooo…. Now you ladies know that response, and what it does to us.

As the red flags went up, I tried not to over think it too much.

After all, we were in therapy for the past two to three years, he was very involved in the church we were a part of at the time, and we were friends with many other couples who looked up to us both and were impressed by the growth we made in our relationship and used our lives as an example to how they should pattern theirs.

So, it never dawned on me that anything was happening in any area, especially not cheating, because we both had a lot to lose, and also, after the major incidents that happened a few years back after that adultery, he promised that it would never happen again.

We got to the Dinner a little early, and I helped the coordinator put things together a bit until the other guests started arriving. I remember the tight-fitting burgundy dress I was wearing and my long black ponytail swung around the edge of my shoulder.

After all we had been through, not only did I have to look good, but I had to put on a good first impression.

Even if it meant being uncomfortable showing my vitiligo for the first time, at such a formal event. I wasn't going to let it keep me from being there and making my presence as 'the wife' known. On top of that, I was not about to let any of his friends see that I was insecure about my condition.

Half way through the dinner, this very kind woman came up to us, and extended her hand to me and looked at him with a smile saying 'So you're not going to introduce me to your wife?'

I was so flattered and impressed, I thought to myself, this is different, a female that he knows that's actually being kind to me, without being in my inbox messaging me about 'what my man is doing.' I told him how I found her to be a nice person, and he shrugged it off.

We made it through the night, I made friends with some of the other wives, and finally for the first time in a long time in our relationship, I felt like I could rest and just be a wife.

My kids were at home, I was out with my husband, and I was doing what usual couples do when they're on a date night.

Before I left, I ran to the bathroom with another wife, and in the bathroom was the same kind lady. As I stepped in, she and the other person she was in the bathroom with, stopped chatting. I figured they didn't want us to hear their conversation, but I could feel the stares of her friend, looking at me from head to toe, almost as if she was annoyed by me being there. I brushed it off as maybe it was just her personality, went back inside and we packed up and left.

Months went by and I found that he would be working later

than usual. I had just had my second surgery done, and was at home off my feet still managing to see about our two girls and do things around the home, but thankfully I was relieved from the office duties, as I healed.

One day, I noticed a familiar number constantly popping up with calls and text messages on his cell phone. Another day, same number, and another day, same number with missed calls whenever he was home, but answered calls when he was at work. I started to 'investigate' and found out that it was in fact the same 'kind' lady that he was talking to outside of working hours.

He explained to me that she was dealing with a rough break up, and that he was just giving her advice, with one particular message from her telling him; 'Thank you for the spiritual advice.'

At this time, we were still in counselling and he had started expressing that he was not sure if he wanted the marriage again, at this time and he was confused.

This not only shattered me to pieces, because I had already cancelled a divorce one time, following the previous incident of adultery, also I would have also taken him back after my dad got involved and my family had sworn to not get involved again. Now here he is suddenly saying, he's unhappy.

I took it all as maybe he was just going through another challenge, and believed him that it was nothing more than him giving her 'spiritual advice' as he put it, and nothing more.

That same year, Trinidad faced a massive flood that ravaged many communities including ours. We thankfully weren't at home at the time, but lost almost everything in our home, due to the floods.

Family, friends, members of our local church and even strangers came together and gave support to us and many other people during that time. Following the floods, we held a thanksgiving at our home to give thanks for all God had saved us from that year, as well as to celebrate our wedding anniversary together with family and friends.

That night, in the middle of the celebration, he offered to take one of my friends home as she had to leave. He didn't return until a few hours later, even though where she was dropping off was like 20 mins away.

When he got back, I questioned him, in tears, embarrassed that my relatives and friends had to see this happening all over again after all this time, and now that we had two daughters being dragged along in it.

He got upset, yelled at me and called me insecure, unable to give a real explanation as to where he was. His lack of an excuse was enough for me to put the pieces of the puzzle that I was already putting together.

I kept on doing what we were advised to do in counselling, praying, fasting, and not only what we were advised in counselling but what I knew best, in the cycle of toxic patterns and behaviors that I had adapted to seasonally throughout the years.

I had noticed that during certain times of the year it was when he would act up more, and I was not sure if it was because of a spiritual demonic cycle or spiritual attack. Or, if it was simply his lack of boundaries and accountability for the fact that he falls into the arms of other women, or they in his whenever we are in a new environment or in a rough patch or season of pressure in our lives. For example the holidays when we are busy doing tasks around the home etc.

Here I was, skin changing, mental health a mess, out of a job, recovering from an injury, my children growing up seeing me unhappy, and now dealing with yet another incident of adultery in only just five years of marriage, and these were the ones that I knew about.

But I stayed.

People ask me all the time, why didn't you get out then. You had all the reasons too, but I couldn't.

For one, I was afraid that I would fall flat on my face financially. I had dreams that one day we would be in ministry together. I was ashamed ; that after I bragged to people about how much my husband had changed, that I now had to reveal to them that It wasn't always so.

I now had two daughters invested in this relationship. One of which was getting ready to write her exams to head into Secondary School.

He was also very loved by men, and each time I would seek counsel, it would end in me being told how much I need to pray more or how much this was an attack on our purpose, leaving me stuck between letting go of 'perceived purpose' and not having to lose my mind.

Now, don't get me wrong, I am all in agreement with the power of prayer. And like God did for Solomon, he can give any man a new heart before he appoints them King. Or brings them into their purpose.

But, we need to teach our daughters and young women that it's also not any 'wives' responsibility to sit around and wait for her husband to reach these pillars in their lives, while she slowly twindles away the seam of who she is and who she can become.

I am sure, that each person reading this now, or will read this, knows at least one woman, who waited her entire life for her spouse to change, and even vice versa, many men also wait for their spouses to change too, often because they married hoping that marriage would somehow be the magic wand that changes it all.

But the reality is, renewing the heart and mind, In preparation for the call God has on our lives, can only happen through true deliverance and real surrender to Christ (as I mentioned before). And a desire to never ever want to go back to our old selves, even if the grass seems greener back there.

Transformation is hard.

But, just like parents must transform a room sometimes to turn it into a nursery to welcome the new born baby.

True purpose filled transformation can only come when we surrender it all to God.

And the evidence of that transformation will be seen in the difficult moments of our lives. It's easy to do the right things when it's all good and nice looking. But, would you remain committed to the things of God when facing persecution? When your wife is injured

> True purpose filled transformation can only come when we surrender it all to God.

and her body changing, will you stay faithful? Will you remain kind to those children when they are getting on your nerves and you had a rough day at work? Will you be gracious to your customers or coworkers when your husband is sleeping with another woman and you found out the night before?

The true essence of our heart is seen when we have all reasons to be mean, or do the wrong things, but we chose to be kind anyways.

The bible says in Luke Chapter 6 that 'Out of an abundance of the heart the mouth speaks'. Therefore, God guides us that we ought to take time to make sure that it's our heart that speaks first, before we even move those lips up or down. Because essentially, what comes out of it, whether in anger, frustration or in a fit of rage, comes from the heart.

A few months into his third affair in our marriage with the 'kind lady'. Our youngest daughter slipped on some water, and fell in the kitchen, passing out for a few minutes.

That evening we were home alone; he was at work and I had just finished giving them dinner. She had spilled some juice on the floor, I mopped it up, and she was running back into the kitchen to get a refill and slipped on the same spot, falling and hitting the back of her head, suffering a mild concussion.

I screamed out to my older daughter at the time to call Daddy and as I was about to pick her up off the floor to run to the car; I heard a knock on the door.

My eldest daughter opened the door thinking it was 'Daddy', when it turned out to be a complete stranger. A colleagueof his, who had come to drop off a document, knocked the door to leave it with me. At the same time my daughter opened it, thinking it was her dad.

When he realized what was happening, he grabbed her from my arms, and placed her in our car. I don't even remember if I was dressed appropriately, nor my daughter. We were probably in our pajamas.

My eldest daughter started praying, and interceded for her sister in the back seat and I put on my hazard lights and I drove to what is usually about a 40 min drive to that hospital, and got there in about 15 mins.

Before we got there, she had regained consciousness and was speaking clearly. She couldn't even remember what happened. My eldest daughter prayed like a prayer warrior from the intercessory group at a church that night.

I had never heard a child pray the way she did for her sister that night. I believe she saved her sister from any further injury just by her prayers. Psalm 127 says that children are a heritage from the Lord. Her name which I discovered later after naming her was 'From the Lord'. And indeed she is.

That experience showed me that God was preparing me to handle crises. Not only was I able to jump into action and care for my child without panicking, but it was like something took over me. A strength that I didn't know I had. All I knew was that I needed to attend to my baby, and get her to where she needed to be.

God prepared me.

When we got to the hospital, we called and called my husband, till eventually he showed up, confirming that the colleague called him to tell him what had happened.

It turned out that that night he was at the other woman's home. And that they were also already intimate with each other.

He met us in the emergency room, and started yelling at me as I broke down crying when he walked in. It was like I felt because he arrived, I no longer needed to be strong, I could be weak now and cry, this was a lot, my baby was hurt and I needed someone to hold me and say everything will be ok.

He told me to 'Hush my mouth, and relax myself', my eldest daughter looked on, as though she too was disappointed. 'Had he not known what we just went through?'

Several tests were run. And everything came back negative. The doctors confirmed that she had suffered a very mild concussion and that we could go home by the next morning. My mother and step dad came, comforted my eldest daughter, and her father took her home.

That night taught me some valuable lessons that I held onto. And still do.

One, that my children and I are resilient, women are strong!

Even though we don't want to be. The world we live in now, sin and unfortunately some men not taking care of us the way we are supposed to be. Has made us have to be stronger than we should need to be at times.

Two, No weapon that is formed against me shall prosper.

It is no coincidence that happened when he was at the other woman's home. The devil and his devices are real, and the truth is, if we play with fire, we open doors for us and those around us to be in the pathway for being burnt.

Praying over your children specifically is so important, because the truth is, we live in a world where people will not like us and our kids, simply because they are 'yours'. And the enemy will not like them, simply because they have purpose!

And three, That God will send even a stranger to help me, in my time of need.

The colleague who showed up to help me when my husband would not answer the phone. Had never been to our home before. A while later, I found out that He was told he could put the letter in the mailbox, but 'something' told him to come up to the porch and knock on the door.

When he did that, my daughter opened it thinking it was her dad in the haste and urgency of what we were dealing with. He was obedient to that tiny voice that told him to give the letter to me personally, to hand over to my then husband. And through his obedience, he helped me get into the car and to the hospital and with a situation that who knows, may have been different if he didn't.

My dear sisters.

God prepares everything for us, before we even see it. He knows what will come our way, and what we will need. Yes, we may want to put things together our own way, and fix our items the way we see fit for when our purpose arrives.

But, most times, what we expect, is never what God has planned.

We have to be willing to let go of our own plans, and allow God to do what he has to do in our lives with HIS Plans, and abandon our own.

Only then will we see the perfecting of his work in us. You have to learn to let go, and let God chart the course of your destiny.

> We have to be willing to let go of our own plans, and allow God to do what he has to do in our lives with HIS Plans, and abandon our own.

7

READY, BUT NOT YET READY!

"If you're not ready to die for it, put the word 'freedom' out of your vocabulary."

Malcolm X

Growing up in a small Caribbean country, with just about 1.4million people. Becoming someone 'great' was not always at the top of everyone's list.

Especially if you did not come from the social classes of the Syrian families that hailed from west Port of Spain, or your family was not into politics or inherited businesses, chances are you would live a pretty ordinary life.

For many, the highest aspirations were to become a doctor or a lawyer, or even a pilot. For me, like I mentioned earlier, my dream was to become a flight attendant. I remember being a child and seeing the airlines flying over our home as they took off, and dreamt that one day I would be able to escape to a world unknown, that I had never seen in real life, apart from on television, or the stories I would hear from strangers or relatives.

At age 16, I got the opportunity to visit my sister at her and her family's home in the U.S, and was even able to volunteer at a local hospital where she worked for some time. This tweaked my interest in the world even more.

When I finally landed my career as a flight attendant, one at first with an airline where I lived in Antigua for close to a year, and the other where I served for 5 years before being injured.

I thought that this was it. The best of both worlds. I got to travel as my job, to be paid to do what I love. And my family, especially my children, will know what it was like to travel around the world for basically free, whenever they wanted.

It was the one thing I wanted, and love the most in my life.

After my injury, and going through the years of being at home dealing with recovering and relearning how to function from being off my feet at times, dealing with the emotional; turmoil that came from not only the job situation but the reality that my husband had once again had an affair, at a time when I was at my lowest.

And also, now having to face a skin condition that was changing my life and my personality forever.

I was exhausted.

And just when I thought it could not get any harder. Came COVID 19.

The pandemic changed so many things for many of us, for me. It opened my eyes to the lie I was living for years. Which was, that I was ok. When I wasn't.

Following finding out, after seeing photos of the person in

our vehicle, and him confessing eventually to everything. I filed for divorce for a second time. Then, after tears, begging and counsel… again, I cancelled it.

My eldest daughter was waiting to write her exams. And to be honest, I made that, yet another excuse as to why I needed to keep the family together.

Even though I was suffering mentally, having nightmares, feeling literally dirty every time I was intimate with my husband, and facing spiritual battles as I worked on my own, to fight through the trauma of the things I was going through, and been through.

I did not think I could bring these feelings or the fact that I was standing on the edge of suicide to anyone, I felt like I was losing my mind. But I couldn't share these feelings with many people.

Because, to people on the outside I looked happy, I looked free. And I looked like I was winning.

During all of this, I held my very first women's event In Trinidad. Was finally at a place where I was embracing my vitiligo, and I was exuding a new found confidence on the outside.

Yet something was missing.

I made the decision to reconcile the marriage after much begging and pleading on his part. Even having him submit to doing an HIV test, as the person who he had been having this at work affair with, had quite a colorful past.

Even though we did a test and they came back negative. For months, into years following our reconciliation, I felt sick each time we had to be intimate. I was told by Christian counsellors that I was 'Not to withhold sex from my husband' as this would lead him into the arms of another woman.

Even though each time we had sex. I would feel a part of me leave.

My motivation for work, parenting, my entrepreneurial dreams, studies, writing, everything that I was once passionate about dwindled day by day.

It plummeted me into a deep dark depression, that left me hopeless with the only motivation to get up each day being my daughters.

One particular night, I glanced over to the bottle of sleeping pills, which I had now become reliant on to sleep every night. And considered taking them all.

Before I leaned over to grab it, a vision came before me of my eldest daughter walking into the room the morning after waking up, and she was the first to find me.

Immediately I rebuked the thought, as the very thought of hurting her like that, and leaving them before my time on this earth with them was complete. Scared, saddened and disgusted me, that I allowed myself to get to this point.

I kept seeking counsel, from many trusted Christian and Psychological counsellors. I realized that I was in fact going through a very real period of depression. Yet no one in my home even knew it. Because I functioned like normal to them. And, with a simple drink of wine each night.

Like many Christian women, we feel at times like it's our duty to carry the weight of the world.

I'll be ok to function again another day.

Like many Christian women, we feel at times like it's our duty to carry the weight of the world.

Unfortunately, we've operated in a backward motion for generations, with women carrying many burdens that we simply were not designed to carry. Leaving us, tired and burnt out.

Suicide, depression, substance abuse and other mental health issues; does not stop at the door step of Christian women, just because we pray or play worship songs each morning.

There is a very real stigma surrounding mental illness in the church, particularly around Christian women, as we are often considered the backbone of the family. Thrusted into the responsibility for being the head intercessor for the home and even other people's homes at times while still fighting to manage to keep our own heads above water.

Christian women find it hard at times to talk about their mental health issues with leaders or even in inner circles, as at times they are told it may be demonic, 'over thinking', 'all in their head' etc.

Without even taking the time to understand the genetic function of the human brain, and how things like stress, and Post Traumatic stress, can have long term impacts on a person's brain, and at times they may need medicine to help combat these issues and regulate what has been disrupted in their brains to be able to feel 'normal' again, and doing so does not make them a 'Lukewarm' Christian.

If you are a woman reading this, and struggling with finding joy in the things that you do, you may have been through a challenging time. Be gentle with yourself.

God is not punishing you; The devil is not always attacking

you. Sometimes, you may need to seek professional help. Sometimes all you need to learn is a little word called 'No.'

Make the right choices to preserve your mental health, distance yourself from some people if you need it, delete the apps you need to. Stop internalizing all the negative self-talk, or trauma you may have faced as a child. And also, there is no need to walk around pretending to be happy every day.

This pandemic has taught us that we have many things in common. Know that you are not alone.

There are millions of other Christian, and non-Christian women just like you. Who loves Jesus dearly, who gets up and intercedes, who fast, who tears down the forces of darkness.. And still struggle with what life may have to bring their way.

It does not make you luke warm, nor does it make you less called by God to produce greatness.

After my flying career ended, I was offered a permanent position in the company in another field. But, I knew, in my gut, that the season had ended.

I'm not going to lie to you, I wrestled with God. I cried many nights asking God why he would take away the one thing that I thought defined me, the one thing that I wanted from him and here he was asking me to let it go.

And I'll never forget, The Holy Spirit said to me 'I need you to give it up, because where I am taking you, no one must say you got there because of them. They must ONLY see ME!'

What I didn't realize is that for years I idolized a glitzy

career. I pulled my suitcase in the airport head held high, hoping I would meet someone that I knew that day, so I could show off where I had arrived in life.

Using it as a way to find peace in my life. Missing church and corporate worship so I could go have fun, dine out and visit parties and strip clubs with the rest of the crew. And have endless alcohol at my disposal if I wanted to.

I had made this job define me. I had made it, just like my relationship with a God in my life.

And God had said. It was time, whether I was ready or not. To let it go, as where he was taking me, there would be NO other God before me but HIM.

I eventually resigned.

When the day came for me to hand over my Company items etc., I looked at the date that I had joined the company. And it read 2011. Exactly 10 years since I joined.

I smiled, and the peace that overcame me was as if I knew God was intentionally setting me up for the next season of my life in the most protective way. I had spent a decade in one place, and now he was ready to take me into another.

Just that this time, I was blindfolded with no idea where I was going. These are the best times for God to do the impossible. When we cannot see or control our outcomes.

I was scared, very scared. Here I would be without a job, in a pandemic. Telling people if they asked me why I left. 'God said to me that the season had ended'... There, people will surely now think I am insane .

But, if you've ever had God give you an instruction, you would know that it is almost impossible to ignore it.

It's like an actual scolding that causes you to think about everything that can and will go wrong if we disobey, and the courage that you get knowing that it's from God and that you know he will not take anything away from you, to give you less.

When I revealed to my husband that I was leaving, he was not the most excited. He looked at me and said, 'If you do that, just don't ask me for anything.'

Again, I was left defenseless to manage my emotions on my own, through what he did not know was the most difficult decision I ever had to make.

I was literally giving up not only the safety of having a stable stream of financial provision in my life. But I was also giving up a childhood dream of mine, which was to travel the world and meet people of many nations.

His response, though just a few words. Hit me harder than any of the physical blows he had ever dealt to me.

Instantly I replayed in my mind, all the times I had stuck with him throughout everything we had gone through together. And yet here I was, left to make this decision on my own.

I'm not sure why I needed his validation. As a wife I know I did. And the little girl inside me who needed the approval of a man and father to tell her. 'Do what you need to do, and I will be here for you!'

I didn't have that in the physical. But in the spirit I had it, I felt it, and I walked boldly into it.

The day I had my exit interview with the manager, she asked me. So, what now? Unsure what even to say to her myself. I said, I'm not sure. I will leave it up to God.

She looked at me from the other side of the virtual screen and spoke. 'Maybe you could write a book.'

I had never shared this with her, that I wrote, or that I had started writing the very book you are reading today already.. and that I had started talks with the publishing company the week before.

Her words were what God knew I needed to hear, to confirm that even though people may not have understood what I was doing.

I was often told; I could have taken the company to court... Why didn't I take the job and the benefits? Didn't I deserve more than this from them?? After all they had done and caused me?? I was making a decision that I didn't even understand. But I heard the Lord say, 'Let it Go!'

But, What if this was all in my head?

God knew my concerns. The depths of my heart. And the things I was afraid of.

He allowed me to hear those words from her, of something that no one knew but him and I. So, I could be reminded that even though I wasn't ready yet to push. That he was there with me holding my hand.

And that I was getting ready to push something out that even I couldn't imagine.

That he was holding my hand, as I was about to come out of my season of pain and labour, and transition into my season of purpose, power, abundance and Love.

LABOUR

"When I was in Labour and I said I don't know how I was going to push one last time, and I did. That's when my baby came out."

Akenna Kublal

The thought of aborting my purpose, makes me anxiously afraid. I know, we are supposed to operate under the realm of 'faith over fear', and knowing who we are and whose we are. But I can tell you, the one thing that brings me the most fear today, is aborting the plans that God had for my life, before I was able to walk into them. As well as my children doing the same, or me doing the same to them by my failure to act, or make certain choices.

Not long after my husband told me he would not support my decision to walk away from the job I loved so dearly. I filed for a divorce. And this time, I stuck to it.

It did not come easily. It came with much doubt. Much fear, much questions that I was going to 'mess up my children', much quoting of scripture by persons who tried to persuade me to stay, even after.

Many saw, and some didn't see what I endured. The years of trauma and difficulties I had been through.

As my children grew more vocal as young women. And I realized the fragility of life caused by this global pandemic. I realized that I needed to stop just existing, and start truly LIVING.

That it was not my duty to construct my life, to help build the foundation of anyone else. And that while God may send me to help people get to their purpose, as he had and still is sending people into mine, it should not come at a cost to your well-being and physical or mental health.

I saw an image of a woman during the Covid 19 pandemic. Trying to juggle it all, cooking dinner, in a Zoom meeting, doing homework, breast feeding the baby, putting out lingerie for the husband when he gets home, packing groceries in the cupboard, with her messy hair and wearing ragged clothing.

As mothers, wives, business women, young ladies in college, we place a lot of emphasis on being busy, on how 'being used', or having things to do is a badge of honor.

But how purposeful is it, if the things that you place so much emphasis on, and all your energies into, come at a detrimental cost to your health.

My Labour, for years, came at a cost to me. When a farmer is working in the field, his Labour goes into tending to the crops that would produce the fruit or vegetables that he sows. When a woman is in Labour, she pushes, with everything she has, to get that baby, that fruit of her womb, out into the world, to bring forth the breath and purpose to which the baby was intended.

For many years of my life, I thought that being busy, looking pretty, acting as a trophy wife and mother, meant that I was being purposeful. And, while we would have achieved much, my children would have as well, and God had been gracious to us.

The reality is, people often see your Glory, but rarely would they get the chance to see or even a glimpse of hearing your story.

And maybe that's God's intention for some of us. Maybe the impact of the Glory on your life, is so great, that God would not dare, anyone see the behind the scenes it took to get you to Labour, because had they seen, they would have assumed it was by your doing, or the doing of mere men and women.

It is in your weakness, to be able to do the things that you have done. To be able to get up each day, and serve your family. To be able to keep praying for your spouse or your children, or to be able to keep serving on that job, when you know those people don't appreciate what you do. It's the very reason why God chose you!

He chose you, because in the midst of your trials, you never gave up. When people said you couldn't do it, but that still small voice whispered to you that you 'can', you kept pushing through.

You kept pushing until your baby was crowning.

When you felt like aborting, and maybe even you did once or twice or 20 times, abort your purpose, You ran back to your Heavenly Father, and he forgave you, because that's what he does.

Even when we abort the things he gives us, he doesn't cancel our inheritance as his children.

God's plans for our life, and his word spoken over the destiny of you and your lineage, cannot be cancelled. No demon in hell, no envious eyes, no friends who abandon you, or jobs that let you go, or even people you Loved who mishandled your heart. Can cancel the anointing on your life.

No grief, no divorce, no loss of a loved one, or diagnosis can stop what God has said yes to in you and your children's life. Stop believing the lie that your purpose is tied into what you 'Can' do, God does not need you to do anything, but Push!

My dear sister, Push. Push like you have never pushed before.

This last push will take some extra effort. Your birth coach will tell you to keep pushing and you'll feel like you can't do it anymore.

But just when you think, you can't go again. That's when you'll know. It's time!

Your labour season will feel like a cross over. A transition from one place to another. The beginning of the next half of your life..

Like Abraham, who left his Father's home, and only through that push to leave, he was able to walk into his new season of abundance. So too, will your final push, take you and your children, and your children's children, into the destiny and purpose to which God has placed under your name and bloodline.

And even them, the people who mishandled you, will benefit, that will be your test.

How will you treat those who mishandled you during your journey, will you chase them away? Or, will you show them the mercy and grace that your Father has shown you.

Your purpose is not just for you. God did not reserve your purpose for you, because you met a certain look, or had the qualifications he needed.

He called you, because you were unqualified, because he could trust you to be humble enough for him to give you the knowledge, and also so you could put in the work, to study to show yourselves approved. That you would sow into his kingdom, and pay your tithes, and be generous to the poor, and take care of your elderly parents, when your siblings may not even consider you the worthy one.

He chose you, the one that the builders rejected, to be the head cornerstone…because you trusted him with your life. You trusted him, and you Loved, even when you weren't trusted by others yourself.

I encourage you, that as you hold that baby, as your very life, the anointing and the gifts God placed into your very being, that you will use your life's journey, your story, to bring change to your family and the world.

That you would never forget your journey from pain to purpose, and that you would forget the old, but remember always with a humble heart, how much you could not have done it alone. Because we both know it was hard.

Oh, so very very hard. But you, my dear sister, have made it, and will keep on making it.

Sometimes love requires us to be to others, what we didn't have.

And that's a hard, and painful thing to do. And it starts with you loving yourself, better than the way others would have loved you.

Being to you, what no one else was. Being kind, loving, gentle, compassionate, choosing yourself, loving YOU, extending the same grace you give to others, to you first.

True love starts with the way you love you. It's hard. I know. But sis. That's what it is.

That is the Labour of Love.

And once you tap into it, I encourage you, don't keep that good news for yourself.

Find another sister, or groups of them, as God has allowed me to, and share this with them, share your story, don't be afraid.

> Your story, your love, your acceptance. Maybe, what another woman is waiting for today, to be set free.

Your story, your love, your acceptance. Maybe, what another woman is waiting for today, to be set free.

My beautiful friend and sister, There was purpose in your pain, walk boldly into it. Raise your head, keep walking into your purpose as you run into the arms of your father. And don't you dare look back.

"God is not unjust; he will not forget your work and the love you have shown him as you have helped his people and continue to help them."

Hebrew 6:10

END

ABOUT THE AUTHOR

Akenna Kublal is an Author, Motivational Speaker, Personal Development Consultant and Founder of Labour of Love Women's Empowerment Events & Akenna Kublal Events and Personal Development Agency.

She hails from the twin isle Republic of Trinidad & Tobago, but travels the globe sharing her testimony of overcoming abuse, adultery, childhood traumas and teenage pregnancy as a young Christian woman. She also uses her platform to bring awareness to Vitligo, a rare skin condition that she also has, being diagnosed with in 2016.

Akenna has a heart for helping women see their true worth, and desires that her life would encourage them to keep pushing, as there is purpose in their pain.

With all that she does, and aspires to do. Her greatest accomplishment and joy, is the privilege to be called Mom, by her two beautiful daughters.

She hopes that each woman that reads this book will be inspired to not give up. And to see the value, in their strength as a woman, and their Labours of Love.

Printed in the United States
by Baker & Taylor Publisher Services